INTRODUCTION

TO THE

HISTORY

OF

AFRICAN CIVILIZATION

Volume II
Colonial and Post-Colonial Africa

C. Magbaily Fyle

University Press of America, Inc.
Lanham · New York · Oxford

Contents

Maps

Preface

This second volume of the *Introduction to the History of African Civilization* examines the controversial twentieth century in Africa's history. Its emphasis is on methods and patterns of domination of Africa by the colonial powers and the new methods invented by the western nations for doing the same thing in the post-colonial period. While not denying Africa's share of responsibility for her own problems, this work shifts the focus towards the role of the colonial and post-colonial patterns of control by the great powers for a continued underdevelopment of Africa

This work should be read in conjunction with volume one, for it is impossible to talk about any aspect of African history without being reminded of the body of prejudice against Africa and Africans treated at the beginning of volume one. It is also important to have a sense of Africa's culture history on which colonial rule forcefully implanted western values.

I need to say a word of thanks to the College of Humanities of the Ohio State University for a Special Research Assignment towards the completion of this manuscript. Thanks also go to the Department of African American and African Studies as well as its chair, Dr. Ted McDaniel for providing some of the funding towards the production of the book.

Magbaily Fyle
April, 2001

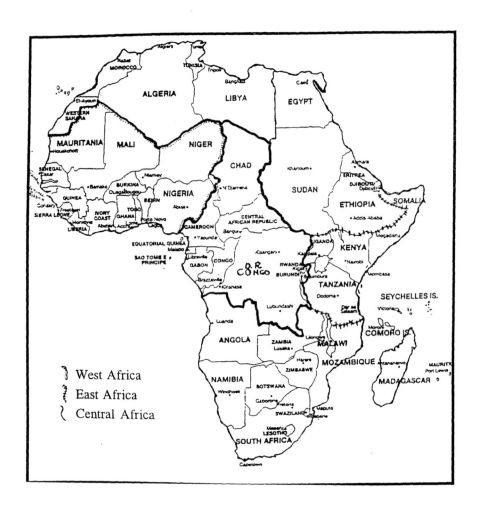

Africa: Political Map

Chapter I

❧∞❧

The Scramble For and Partition of Africa

Background

The last quarter of the nineteenth century could be taken as the period embracing the scramble for Africa. The 'event' is described in this way because European countries, in a bid to outdo each other, literally scrambled to lay claim to every piece of territory in Africa wherever this was possible. The first question that would arise in this regard is why European nations would engage in such a mad rush to acquire territory in Africa.

There are several factors that contributed to a heightening of European interest in African territory by this time. Some of these factors were apparently less directly related to Africa, but did have a role in the ensuing events. For example, rivalry between European nations was sometimes played out in theaters elsewhere. By 1870, the European system was changing rapidly. France, regarded as the primary military power in Europe, had been humiliatingly defeated by Germany as the German Chancellor, Bismark, exploited conflict with France to unite the various German duchies into a large European nation. The emergence of a large, single Germany threatened the European balance of power. Britain, the dominant sea power, thus found herself faced with a new power in Europe while France, nursing her wounds from the defeat, was seeking to demonstrate anywhere else that she still had a lot of power left over. The rivalry between these European powers began to fuel urges for expansion outside Europe. French soldiers began to show more militancy in attacking territory outside Senegal, then one of France's main outposts on the African continent.

The competing interests among European nations played out in arenas other than the balance of power in Europe, and this excited the desire to acquire territory in Africa. The last quarter of the nineteenth century saw an intensification of the industrial revolution with mass production of goods in the other European nations catching up with the initial lead that Britain had in this area. This increased competition in industry among these European countries meant a greater interest in controlling markets to sell their surplus production.

While Britain remained the leading industrial power earlier in the nineteenth century, she pursued a policy of free trade as far as external markets were concerned. This policy was intended to prevent any European nation from interfering with the trade of another in any territory whatsoever. This policy was advantageous to Britain. It meant that Britain could avoid any expensive control of foreign territory needed as markets. Her commanding industrial lead made it possible to dominate such markets and sell her products without having to politically control such areas.

By the late nineteenth century, as rapidly increasing industrial output among the other European nations and the United States threatened, competition for markets became a more serious concern. This competition suggested control of such markets to keep off rivals, a measure usually described as protectionism. Thus where free trade dictated a policy of avoiding control of territory, protectionism indicated the opposite, a need to control such territory and thereby protect them as markets. By the last quarter of the nineteenth century, protectionism, creating the desire for empire, was growing higher on the agenda for Britain and her industrial neighbors. The implications of this for territory in Africa, with whose coastal trade Europeans were by now very familiar, would be immense.

Another contributory factor to the scramble was that there was a growing belief among Europeans that Africa, the continent they knew little about beyond the coastal areas, contained vast untapped resources that could enrich European countries. Huge deposits of diamonds had been discovered at Kimberly in South Africa by 1870 that was to radically alter South African history. Large gold deposits followed in the 1880s. The European nations therefore began to nourish the idea that the heart of Africa held similar treasures and so the first comers would get it all. Each European country therefore wanted to stake its claim to the territories having these potential riches even before such wealth would be uncovered.

Against this background of increasing European interest in controlling territory everywhere, including Africa, we need to consider other factors that would have further encouraged them to venture out to grab colonies in Africa. The most important of such factors was rapid advances in armaments technology. This involved particularly the development by the middle of the nineteenth century of the repeater rifles like the breech loading rifles and more specifically the maxim gun. These arms revolutionized warfare and gave a vast advantage to Europeans in their quest to take over control of Africa.

African countries had been used to buying guns from Europeans, but these were the old Dane guns, to be reloaded after every shot. As the repeater rifle industry exploded by the later nineteenth century, these weapons were kept from African customers by collusion among the European powers, culminating in the Brussels Treaty of 1890 that specifically prohibited the sale of these new arms to African rulers. Of course, it was in the interest of the European countries, all of them involved in the Scramble, not to break this embargo on the sale of repeater rifles. Thus it is important that by the end of the nineteenth century, about the end of the conquest of Africa, not one African ruler had a maxim gun, so decisive in the conquest of African countries.

There were other advances as well in medical technology, for instance, which facilitated the European prey on African territory. For example, the discovery of quinine, a prophylaxis as well as a cure for the deadly malaria inflicted by the anopheles mosquito, had considerably reduced the death toll of Europeans particularly in West Africa.

Factors Leading to the Scramble

The actual territorial disputes leading to the Scramble for Africa occurred on a variety of fronts on this huge continent. It all however amounted to rivalry for territory which quickened as one European country reacted to the claims for territory by the other.

One of the leading actors in this theatre was Leopold, king of Belgium. He had an interest in setting up a personal empire for himself in the heart of Africa and he used every deception to pursue his plan unrestricted by the other European powers and even his own government. He disguised this intent in the name of geographical interest, inviting other European nations to a geographical conference in Brussels in 1876. He simultaneously set up an International African Association ostensibly for related pursuits and sent out explorers like Henry Morton Stanley to 'explore' the area around the Congo River.

Stanley fulfilled this exercise on behalf of Leopold's International African Association, setting up trading posts in the area and signing treaties with local rulers. This gave Leopold the basis to develop his interest in an area too close to where Portuguese traders had been operating. The Portuguese proceeded soon thereafter to claim control of territory in Mozambique where Afro-Portuguese traders had been active. But Portugal was a small and relatively weak country in Europe and needed support for its interest in the area around the Congo River.

Leopold's activities in the Congo area found more ready reaction from France. A French explorer was sent to the area and he signed treaties with local rulers to support French claim to a large area on the north bank of the Congo River. This was only part of the expansionist activity of France in Africa. The French from Senegal were interested in taking control of much of the interior of West Africa and linking up with the Niger area. In 1882, France declared control over Porto Novo, close to the lower Niger, where British traders had long been operating. But the French were also showing greater interest in places like Tunisia in North Africa and the island of Madagascar.

Cooperation between France and Britain became strained after Britain alone occupied Egypt in 1882. As this began to take on the signs of a permanent occupation, it simply heightened France's determination to expand her claims to various portions of Africa. Britain on the other hand saw a good strategy in supporting Portugal's rival claim to the mouth of the Congo River.

All of this happened in the few years between 1879 and 1883. In 1884, the German Chancellor, Bismark, declared 'protectorates' over South West Africa (Namibia), the Cameroons and Togo in West Africa. The heat was growing and, with the German presence in South West Africa, Britain began to grow more restless in the interior of South Africa.

These multifarious claims to territory in Africa were made primarily in terms of proclamations by one European nation at its capital, and subsequent diplomatic maneuvers with other European countries. It was always maintained that these European claims to African territory were based on bilateral treaties with the African rulers concerned. There is no indication that any of the European powers ever questioned any of the treaties the other claimed to have signed with African rulers. They were simply accepted as valid.

Key Areas During the Scramble for Africa

The problems for the historian evaluating these treaties are enormous. It is clear that virtually all of the African rulers signing these treaties spoke no European languages. This would imply that the treaties were finalized through interpreters. Who were these interpreters and what were they interpreting? These issues have never been seriously addressed by historians. All of our information about these treaties comes from the same European sources that were claiming these territories.

African rulers, particularly in coastal areas, had been used to trading with European visitors. These rulers sometimes even allowed these European traders to intervene in settling disputes, apparently regarding them as unbiased arbitrators. It seems most likely that African rulers saw no objection to putting their thumb prints or 'X' marks on pieces of paper brought by their European associates of trading partners; it seems clear that their own cultural values regarding signing away territory were never questioned.

Let us examine one case of treaty signing in southern Africa for which we have adequate documentation. This involved on the one hand the Ndebele kingdom, an offshoot of the political revolution called the *mfecane* in South Africa, and its ruler, Lobengula. On the other, the wealthy, powerful and ambitious Cecil Rhodes was determined at all costs to take control of the area of present day Zimbabwe where Lobengula's Ndebele kingdom was located.

Lobengula's father, Mzilikazi, the previous Ndebele king, had been friends with a British missionary, Robert Moffat, who had been frustrated in his determination to convert the Ndebele to Christianity. Moffat had left Ndebele country in frustration in 1868. Now, in the 1880s, he was eager to support Rhodes' imperial designs over Ndebele country. Rhodes wanted full control of minerals there while taking over all of the area on behalf of Britain.

Moffat's reason for supporting Rhodes was to avenge his failure to convert the Ndebele to Christianity. He wrote that Rhodes' company would eventually conquer and destroy the Ndebele kingdom. Thus his racist arrogance, fueled by vengeance set him on a course of deception of Lobengula. Moffat posed as a spiritual advisor, trying to give friendly advice to an 'old friend.' On this pretext, Moffat deceived Lobengula into believing he was renewing an 1836 treaty signed between the British and the Ndebele by Mzilikazi, the former Ndebele king. What Lobengula actually signed was a familiar British treaty in Africa by the late 1880s, that he would keep all other European powers except the British from his territory. In terms of negotiations between the European powers, this treaty meant virtual acceptance of British colonial rule and this signaled the British occupation of what became Rhodesia.

But Rhodes was not satisfied merely with British control of Lobengula's territory. He wanted full control of the mineral rich area for his company. Thus another treaty was needed with Lobengula. Rhodes then sent further agents led by Charles Rudd to get this monopolistic agreement from Lobengula. Moffat was sent ahead to condition Lobengula for the visit of this team led by Rudd. Deceiving Lobengula into believing that he was merely a man of God, Moffat introduced Rudd and his party as 'honourable and upright men.' By a combination of deceit and misrepresentation, Moffat and the party led by Rudd got Lobengula to sign the Rudd concession by the end of 1888 which gave Rhodes full control of Lobengula's country. Verbal commitments made by the Rudd party that were advantageous to Lobengula were not included in the treaty. In a society where the verbal commitments were in fact more important than written documents, Lobengula would not have seen the problem there. He was only to be informed later when he protested that verbal statements were invalid. Rhodes used this treaty to occupy the neighboring Shona country in 1890. Lobengula later found out what he had signed and attempted to repudiate the treaty in a newspaper in neighboring Bechuanaland. But it was too late.

Thus the argument that African rulers gave up their territory in these treaties is most certainly out of the question. In fact Frederick Lugard, one of the major architects in establishing British imperialism in Africa wrote in his diary a statement typical of all of those treaties. He was referring to the treaties signed between the Kabaka of Buganda and the agents of the Imperial British East Africa Company. He mused:

> No man if he understood would sign it, and to say that a savage chief had been told that he cedes all [sovereign] rights to the company in exchange for nothing is an obvious untruth. If he had been told that the company will protect him against his enemies, and share in his wars as an ally, he has been told a lie, for the Company have no idea of doing any such thing....

A number of these British treaties that have survived were actually treaties of friendship that, by the 1890s, had the familiar clause of not conceding territory to any other European country. These friendship treaties were used to claim territory. We therefore cannot talk about treaties related to European claims to territory during the Scramble. The act of sending an explorer to an area and his return with pieces of paper claimed to be treaties

MOROCCO
TUNISIA
SPANISH SAHARA
ALGERIA
LIBYA
EGYPT
0   500
Miles
ERITREA   FRENCH SOMALILAND
GAMBIA
FRENCH WEST AFRICA
ANGLO-EGYPTIAN SUDAN
(condominium)
BRITISH SOMALILAND
PORTUGUESE GUINEA
NORTHERN NIGERIA
EMPIRE OF ETHIOPIA
SIERRA LEONE
SOUTHERN
LIBERIA
GOLD COAST
TOGOLAND
CAMEROONS
FRENCH EQUATORIAL AFRICA
SPANISH GUINEA
UGANDA
BRITISH EAST AFRICA
ITALIAN SOMALILAND
BELGIAN CONGO
GERMAN EAST AFRICA
CABINDA
ANGOLA
NORTHERN RHODESIA
NYASALAND
SOUTH WEST AFRICA
SOUTHERN RHODESIA
MOZAMBIQUE
BECHUANALAND
UNION OF SOUTH AFRICA
SWAZILAND
BASUTOLAND

Portuguese
British
British-occupied
French
Belgian
German
Spanish
Italian

Colonized Territories in Africa by 1910

was however enough to form the basis of negotiation for African territory between the European powers in complete disregard of the African rulers.

Treaty making however proceeded apace and by the 1890s, African rulers had somehow caught on with the deception of the treaties and some sought to use the process to their own advantage, to manipulate rival European interests or seek help against internal enemies. In spite of the predominance of treaties, many of the African peoples did not sign any treaties at all at any point in the process. The Koranko rulers of Sierra Leone, largely acephalous peoples, never signed any treaties until the drawing of boundaries and the new administration signaled to them that they had become British colonial subjects.

As the tension over rival claims to African territory heated, Bismark, the German ruler, picked up on a suggestion earlier made by Portugal that a conference be held on Africa to settle disputed issues. This conference met in Berlin late in 1884. As the conference was decided upon, the European powers scrambled to obtain paper claims to virtually all African territory as it was obvious that negotiations were going to be held based on those claims. The Berlin Conference in this way intensified the scramble for Africa.

The two main decisions at the conference involved the bases for claim to territory in Africa and the means of establishing proof of authority over the claimed areas. The first referred to as the "spheres of influence" clause, provided procedures for notifying the European powers about claims to territory for 'proper' ratification of such claims. But this clause also indicated that if a European country claimed the coast, the uninterrupted hinterland could be added on to it!

More significantly, the second major clause on effective occupation insisted on a demonstration of authority in the territory claimed by any European power in order that proper controls would be exercised. This effective occupation clause therefore meant that European nations had to make good their paper claims to territory by physically taking control of such claimed areas. Hitherto, most of the claims were just that, and involved agreements between European powers without the involvement of the African societies concerned. Effective occupation was to bring Europeans to take control of African countries and the conquest of Africa was thus ushered in.

The Partition

The dividing up of African territory continued apace after the Berlin conference. This was usually done by bilateral negotiations between

European countries who needed to settle any boundary between their contiguous territorial claims. In the end, by the beginning of the twentieth century, a map of Africa emerged identifying the entire continent, apart from Ethiopia and Liberia, as European colonial territories.

The new boundaries between these colonies were for the most part arbitrary. Some thirty to forty percent of the borders followed lines of longitude and latitude, irrespective of where the lines cut through. As one informant put, "I was a child when the boundary was drawn. It fell on our house. If you were in the front entrance, you were in Sierra Leone. If you were at the back, you were in Guinea.' Other boundaries followed natural phenomena like mountains, mostly rivers. Borders cut across ethnic groups and settlements leaving close relations divided between French, English, Portuguese or German systems. There was some consideration in a few areas for existing African political systems, where this fit into the rival claims and settlements made between the European powers. But this was generally not a serious consideration.

Whether this partition and new borders have been good or bad for African peoples have been issues for serious debate. It is, for example, indicated in some quarters that the solidifying by the colonial powers of fluid borders that had existed between some African polities was a positive and progressive factor. While this may be so, one can hardly defend the arbitrariness of the imposition of most of the borders with regard to the lives and future of the peoples divided by such new frontiers.

Questions

1. To what extent did rivalry between the European powers contribute to the scramble for Africa?
2. Discuss the significance of bilateral treaties in the claim to African territory by the European powers.

Chapter II

ഇൻ

Resistance to the Imposition of Colonial Rule

The conquest of Africa could not have come at a more inopportune time for African peoples, but the circumstances were highly favorable to the European nations. In the first place, the European nations had a carefully concerted plan to take over control of all of these African societies. The plan was coordinated to the point of the signing of a convention in Brussels in 1890 to deny the sale of arms to African rulers and peoples. The European nations had technological superiority, particularly the maxim gun, a canon so powerful by the standards of the time, that it instilled tremendous confidence in the European led forces invading the continent, and wreaked havoc in the African armies defending their sovereignty.

The last quarter of the nineteenth century was also a period of peace in Europe so that the European countries could more readily iron out disputes relating to the conquest of Africa. The industrial revolution had also provided ample resources which, with the absence of war in Europe, could be deployed to the African venture.

The African peoples were not so fortunate. The plan with which the Europeans were armed to come and conquer their lands was completely unknown to them, or this would have suggested reasons for greater cooperation among the African societies. But worse, this was a period of political expansion and consolidation of states in many parts of Africa, particularly in West Africa. Such activity involves antagonisms between neighboring units as well as those being brought into the orbits of these expanding states. In such situations, neighboring peoples were looking for allies who were not necessarily their neighbors, and this is the way most of the invading Europeans were perceived by the African rulers in the period of the conquest, until the African rulers came to realize what was happening. They mostly only found out their grave error in calculation after it was too late.

Another important factor was the fact that most African peoples were organized politically into small political units hardly above the level of a single settlement. These, often referred to as acephalous societies, had worked well in the political arrangements of the times before European conquest. In the face of enemies with vastly superior weapons and a concerted plan, such small scale units proved detrimental to resistance. We shall see that attempts to coordinate resistance over several of these political units took considerable time, planning, and secrecy in the face of the European onslaught.

Patterns of Resistance

While there were various forms of responses to the incoming imperial conquest, all of these responses were united with one goal. They were devising ways of preserving their independence against European incursion, as this became apparent. Methods of achieving this varied owing to a number of factors. These had to do with the nature of the European advance, or of existing political relations between neighbors; there was also the issue of the size of political units, for with centralized kingdoms, responses were generally determined by the rulers. The existence of common cultural bonds among neighbors with small-scale political units offered opportunities in some cases to mobilize different ethnic and political groups.

Significantly important also were those groups that have been labeled as collaborators. These have been praised by colonialists as having foresight and were the winners, but were equally condemned by new African nationalists as sell-outs. Since the goal of all groups was to preserve their independence, those groups that sought collaboration with the European imperialists were also trying to maintain their sovereignty. Thus they were sometimes seeking limited cooperation to get rid of an old enemy, unaware that they were by that process giving up sovereignty. Some collaborated initially and joined European imperial armies, only to rebel later when they realized they had by that process relinquished their authority. There were a few who knowingly collaborated; but they must have obviously thought that there was a way of wiggling out of such commitments and thereby retaining control of their territory.

While some of these forms of resistance were rewarded with initial successes, the decisive fire power of the Europeans eventually won the day. It was only in Ethiopia that the Ethiopian army scored a decisive defeat of the Italian imperialists who did not have the spirit to return immediately. Let us look at these forms of resistance in turn.

Military Resistance to Incoming Colonizers

By far the majority of initial responses to the European led imperial armies involved immediate military confrontation to prevent the colonial take-over. This was obvious in spite of the overwhelming advantage the Europeans had in weaponry. In present day Malawi, Mwase Kasungu led the forces of his Chewa people against the British in 1896; he committed suicide rather than face capture. In the area of today's Angola, the Humbe and Biha peoples attacked Portuguese forces trying to set up ports of control in their territory.

The Nandi ethnic group of Kenya took up arms when the British tried to build a railway through their territory, for it was with such measures that many groups came to realize the reality of colonial rule. The Nandi were politically organized in territorial units called *pororiet*. Their military units were spread over a number of these *pororiet* because these units were based on cultural ties like age sets that were common to a number of these *pororiet*. These military units were thus the equivalent of standing armies uniting the military potential of a number of political units. The Nandi used this to put up stout resistance to the British in the 1890s and were only broken by the murder of their leader by British commanders in 1905.

In the Tanzanian hinterland, ethnic groups like the Mbungu and the Hehe fought the Germans in the 1890s. Some like the Hehe scored initial victories against the German forces in 1891, killing about 290 of them. They were only defeated four years later. Similarly in Uganda, Kabarega, the ruler of the kingdom of Bunyoro and the British clashed between 1891 and 1899. Unable to defeat the British and with an uncompromising Lugard leading the British forces, Kabarega resorted to guerilla warfare until captured in 1899.

Primary military confrontation was more obvious in West Africa particularly against the French who were more determined to take control of claimed areas by force. French military advance across west Africa from

Senegal followed a more systematic pattern in an attempt to link up with their posts in Niger and Chad and on the coast with Ivory Coast and Dahomey. There had been a tradition of military resistance to French advance which had been evident in the Senegambia area since the mid nineteenth century. This resistance had been buttressed by Islam which enjoined intolerance of the infidel Christian French.

But the French had slowly gained control of a number of areas in the Upper Senegal River area since the 1860s. The *Damel* (king) of Cayor, Lat Dyor, flatly opposed French attempts to build a railway through his territory in the Senegambia region, even in writing. He wrote to the French Governor in Senegal "…as long as I live, be well assured, I shall oppose with all my might the construction of this railway." But his territory was invaded in 1882; he was deposed and Cayor fell under French rule.

In Dahomey, the French declared a 'protectorate' over Porto Novo, a vassal of Dahomey, and moved to occupy Cotonou, one of its towns, in February 1890. The king of Dahomey, Behanzin, mobilized his army, attacked the French garrison and set about destroying palm trees that he believed was part of the French interest. The French agreed to a peace treaty in October 1890 in which Behanzin lost Cotonou, but was recognized as king of Dahomey. The French were only playing for time. Behanzin suspected this and continued to modernize his weaponry, buying what the Germans next door in Togo would sell. But by late 1892, the French attacked again and this time their better armaments prevailed. Starved of supplies, the Dahomey armies disintegrated. The French finally took control after another offensive in 1893.

Early in 1891, the French also launched attacks against the Baule peoples of the Ivory Coast. The Baule fought brilliantly and the French sued for peace in 1892. Again, this was just a temporary measure. Determined Baule resistance ensured that the French would only come back after defeating the Mandinka empire builder, Samori, in 1898.

Strategies of Deception

The French in particular used a variety of methods of deception to be able to succeed in their elaborate scheme to conquer the African territories. Whenever their forces were stretched, they would sue for peace as we have seen in the case of Cayor and Dahomey and the Baule. Such tactics were not unique to the French. The Germans exploited rivalry between the Nama and Herero peoples in southern Africa by offering the Herero an alliance against their Nama enemy. After the Nama were crushed, it was only a matter of time before eventual Herero resistance was quelled. The French also elaborately used this strategy of capitalizing on regional antagonisms between African rulers to secure alliances that enabled them to conquer some areas. One case in point was again in the Senegambia area, around present day Senegal and Gambia.

By the second half of the nineteenth century, Al Hajj Umar, a popular Muslim cleric had created a strong Islamic kingdom in this region among the Tuculour peoples of sedentary Fulbe and Mandinka descent. The French had been signing treaties with Sekou Ahmadu, Umar's successor, as they realized they could not readily defeat him. Sekou Ahmadu was by the 1870s facing strong internal dissention from Bambara, Mandinka and Fulbe units which had been incorporated into his kingdom. Ahmadu therefore was equally in need of treaties with the French that would provide a respite while he dealt with his internal problems. As both sides needed treaties, these were signed between Ahmadu and the French in 1872 and in 1880. By these treaties the French professed to respect Ahmadu's sovereignty as long as he cooperated with the French. Although the French did not quite stick to the terms of the treaties, they gave Ahmadu the breather he needed to face his fractious subjects. The 1880 treaty was in fact more advantageous to the French who used it to prevent an alliance between Ahmadu and Mamadou Lamine, ruler of a neighboring rival kingdom of the Soninke peoples. The French were experiencing serious opposition from Lamine in her bid to dominate this region. Finally with the tacit support of Ahmadu, the French defeated Lamine's Soninke kingdom. But as soon as this was done, the French were now strengthened enough to pounce on Ahmadu and seized his capital in 1890.

In another similar situation, in today's Republic of Guinea, the French signed a treaty with the Fulbe rulers of Futa Jalon to respect their leadership position if they submitted to French rule. This appeared, to many African rulers, a half way decent solution to the alternative of fighting Europeans who had vastly superior weapons. Unfortunately, these African leaders sometimes believed these treaties would be honored. They only found out later, after their rights were completely trampled upon, that the French had as much respect for these treaties as for the paper they were printed on.

Samori Toure

Some African leaders used a combination of diplomacy, alliance and military confrontation and this sometimes gave them an initial edge in the struggle against the incoming European imperialists. Samori Toure, the Mandinka empire builder in the Upper Guinea region, used all of these methods. Samori's empire between northern Sierra Leone and the Ivory Coast, had a well trained and equipped army. He had been able to purchase repeater rifles from the British with whom he had been trading for many yeaars, until the Brussel's convention blocked such arms sales. But he had no heavy artillery like the maxim gun.

When necessary, Samori signed treaties with the French since he realized he could not defeat them outright. At one point in the 1880s, he agreed to place his entire empire under British protection. This was merely a strategy to thwart the French who were determined to destroy him and take over his kingdom. Though his well disciplined army won many battles against the French, he was eventually overwhelmed, pushed back systematically towards the Ivory Coast where he was captured in 1898 after sixteen years of almost constant engagement with the French.

Delayed Resistance

In a number of areas there was no initial military resistance, though this was to erupt later. This was due to a variety of factors. In some regions, particularly close to the coast, African leaders, fearful of the military might of the Europeans, preferred to negotiate in the hope of thereby retaining at least some sovereignty. This element of negotiation, sometimes of outright submission, seemed to have occurred mostly in areas where the might of the advancing imperialists was already known, but where the Europeans came more peacefully, explained to the people some element of the new dispensation of colonial rule and sought concurrence. This concurrence was in some places assumed by the silence of the listeners, many of whom thought it was worth giving a try in the circumstances. They realized only a couple of years later that this was not working. This was when they organized resistance and attempted to drive out the Europeans.

Some rulers deliberately joined the Europeans against oppressive neighbors. Many of these hoped they would still be able to rule their people under the Europeans. It did not turn out the way they had hoped and so they resisted later. In still a few areas with smaller scale polities, there was a need to build up coalition through cultural ties and perception of a common enemy. This involved quite a bit of concession and negotiation that took considerable time and delayed the resistance movement. Let us examine some examples of this delayed resistance.

One prominent area of this delayed resistance was in Leopold's Congo. The local population often considered the agents of the Congo Free State, as it was called, as trading partners and allies in an area where the Arab slave trading had intensified the need for allies and protection. But these same Congo officials soon began to levy taxes and recruit free labor. It was then that the population realized what they were in for. Consequently, between 1885 and 1905 a series of rebellions broke out among the different Congo peoples. The Budja and Bowa peoples revolted about 1900 against forced labor conscription and fought a protracted guerilla warfare against the Belgian Congo rulers for a few years. The Yaka held out in rebellion against the Free State officials for over a decade before they were finally conquered in 1906.

A similar situation was evident in the colony of Sierra Leone where British agents led by Governor Cardew toured the interior in 1895 to explain the new British rule. Their meetings were greeted often by silence which was taken as consent. As the British proceeded to effect their administration and levy taxes, a flood of petitions reached the British headquarters at Freetown complaining about these new measures. Failing to get redress, rebellions erupted in the southern part of the country led by the large Mende ethnic group in April, 1898, and another in the north led by Bai Bure, which involved a coalition of different ethnic groups and polities. The Mende rising was much shorter for lack of a single leader, but Bai Bure's movement lasted almost a whole year before he was defeated by British forces.

In present day Namibia which was initially the German colony of South West Africa, the Herero peoples could only attempt to drive out the Germans when the German troops were away to put down a rebellion elsewhere. One hundred Germans were killed and the Herero destroyed several farms and captured large herds of cattle. When the German troops returned, they wreaked a savage vengeance in which about seventy-five percent of the Herero population of some 70,000 was massacred. A large number of the remainder fled to neighboring Bechuanaland and South Africa. On the Kenya coast the Mazrui family resisted British rule after the British take over initiated British interference in their trading arrangements and in the succession system. Mbaruk bin Rashid organized hit-and-run warfare against well armed British forces; the British had to get reinforcements from Indian troops to defeat Mbaruk.

The *Kabaka* Mwanga of Buganda who ascended the throne in 1894, the same year Uganda was declared a protectorate, attempted a different form of resistance. He was a master at manipulating opposing factions. He had played Muslims against Christian factions at his court in an attempt to retain control and keep off the British. Mwanga planned to revive an old tradition of naval exercises on an island on lake Victoria/Nyanza, as a ruse to get rid of the foreign rulers and their Baganda followers. The British rulers and their Baganda followers who would have landed on the island for the exercise would have been abandoned there. The plan leaked and a revolt led to Mwanga being deposed.

Coalitions for Resistance

We have mentioned earlier that particularly in regions dominated by small scale political systems often involving a single large settlement, there was a need to build up coalitions against the common perceived enemy, the incoming Europeans. In the absence of a wide embracing political system, people had to look to common cultural ties, for such factors provided the basis for cooperation between disparate political units. These common ties could include ritual, involve secret societies or age-grade systems.

It would not have been easy to facilitate such cooperation between groups that may not have cooperated militarily before. And this particularly in the face of European forces known to have decisive military superiority. In such instances the working out of such coalitions was bound to consume considerable time and would have delayed the resistance. Such coalitions needed stronger bonding elements in the face of European arms and this was often provided by religious beliefs.

The Chimurenga

The best known example of this religious phenomenon is the case of the *chimurenga* (war of resistance) among the Shona and Ndebele of present day Zimbabwe. It will be recalled that Rhodes' British South Africa Company had occupied both Matabele (pl. for Ndebele; the '*ma*' is a plural prefix) and Mashona countries by 1892. While the Ndebele had a centralized kingdom, the Shona were scattered in small-scale principalities. But the *chimurenga* erupted almost simultaneously in both areas—in Matabeleland in March 1896 and in Mashonaland in June 1896. Rhodes' forces had largely been away in South Africa. They returned and first tried to settle the Ndebele rising. This was one colonizing force that included perhaps the largest number of Europeans—two thousand of them, while all the other Africans in the force numbered only about six hundred. Failing to defeat the Ndebele by conventional military methods, Rhodes sued for peace rather than face the prospect of the British government taking over and ending his control. The Ndebele, poorly armed and fearing ultimate defeat, agreed to the peace term offers.

Rhodes' forces then turned to the much more diffused Shona *chimurenga*. This was coordinated by traditional priests collectively called *svikiro*. The most prominent of the *svikiro* was an individual named Mkwati who had extended the religious element to the Ndebele rising. In Mashonaland, the prominent *svikiro* was called Kagubi and a female, Nehanda. It is clear that the *svikiro* capitalized on the prevailing hostility towards the imperialists by preaching that the plagues of rinderpest, locusts and drought, as well as forced labor, flogging of adults, house tax, had all been brought by the Europeans. But more significantly the *svikiro* enjoined that *Mwari* or *Mlimo* (respectively the Shona and Ndebele words for 'God') had decreed that the white man had to be driven away. And *Mwari* or *Mlimo* would turn the European's bullets into water.

That this latter injunction which may sound trivial to us was believed by the Ndebele and Shona, should be understood in terms of the power of religion over these peoples. This religious edict provided the galvanizing force and the psychological booster necessary to get the Ndebele and Shona to face the far superior weapons of the Europeans that they already knew about. The *svikiro* had a vast secret network of communications which served to coordinate the uprising and keep the message alive. That the Shona were ultimately defeated piecemeal after a few years should not detract from our understanding of the ability of religion to mobilize in such difficult circumstances. In fact part of the success of the Europeans rested in capturing Kagubi and Nehanda late in 1897 and executing them. But the Europeans were alive to the power wielded by these religious leaders so they buried the *svikiro* secretly "so that no natives would take away their bodies and claim that their spirits had descended to any other prophetess."

There are other examples of the role of religion in these wars of resistance. While there was no clear information of the use of ritual in the Sierra Leone rebellions discussed earlier, it was important enough for the colonial District Commissioner to report to his superior in England that 'medicines were passing to and fro' during the rebellion.

The Maji Maji rebellion of 1905 against the Germans in Tanganyika (Tanzania) was another case in point. Within a few years of German rule, the peoples of Tanzania had been so badly brutalized with wanton killings and extremely harsh forced labor, that they had no alternative but to rebel. This rebellion was led by a prophet called Kinjikitile Ngwale. In pronouncements similar to those of the *svikiro* discussed earlier, Kinjikitile enjoined people of over twenty different ethnic groups to combine against the Germans. He built a large shrine calling it the 'throne of God.' Most importantly he prepared ritual water (*maji*) that had to be drunk by everyone. This, he declared, would make them immune to the white man's bullets. This gave the religiously conscious peoples the signal for determination to face the militarily superior Germans. Even though Kinjikitile was quickly captured and hanged by the Germans, his brother took over the position and the *maji* ceremonies, with the title of Nyamgumi. Again, this did not prevent the Germans from a brutal vengeance on the rebels. But it did demonstrate the power of ritual and the extent of possible cooperation built on hostility towards colonial rule.

Conclusion

It should be clear by now that colonial rule was not welcomed by Africans who did everything in their power and within their abilities to avoid or oppose it. There would have been tiny minorities who welcomed colonial rule, like the westernized Africans of the Sierra Leone colony. By the late nineteenth century, these latter had experienced over a century of British colonization and indoctrination. The alliance of most African rulers with the advancing Europeans should not be taken as embracing colonial rule. If anything, these allies were looking for short term advantage, particularly against powerful neighbors. They quickly realized the folly of their alliance as the sovereignty they thought they could preserve was wrested from them.

Questions

1. Identify and explain the use of cultural factors in the African struggle against the imposition of colonial rule.
2. In what ways did Europeans manipulate African rulers and peoples in order to assume rule over them?

Chapter III

෩෬

Colonial Administrative Systems in Africa Before World War II

There are two major aspects of colonial administration in Africa, particularly before the Second World War. On the one hand, there are indications of a developing, organized policy in some areas, particularly with the French administration in the Senegal area and British administration in general. On the other hand, virtually all of the colonial rulers, including the British, engaged in widespread atrocities in the early phases of their administration, particularly in east, central and southern Africa. Here the demands for forced labor for mining and public works led to a virtual holocaust in central and southern Africa. No organized administration of the colonial peoples could be detected, and what organization existed was limited to methods of the most ruthless exploitation for collecting extremely high taxation, conscripting forced labor and compulsory cultivation. The initial period of colonial administration was however marked by successive rebellions as Africans resisted attempts by the new colonial rulers to establish European authority.

Background Factors

There were certain issues underlying all colonial administrative practice in Africa that need to spelled out at the outset. All European colonialists had an unequivocal belief in the superiority of their race and culture. This dominated their attitudes to every aspect of administration. Thus the way ordinances, laws and policy prescriptions were interpreted and executed by colonial officials was always affected by the fact that the officials felt that Africans were inferior beings and therefore should not usually be given the benefit of a more favorable treatment.

The second point that needs to be made here is that there was little that could be regarded as consistent colonial policy on the part of every European colonizer, particularly in the first twenty years of colonial rule. The dominant element was to maintain firm control and support a policy of extracting commodities from these colonies for the benefit of the colonizer. In this pursuit, certain practices proved more useful than others. Whatever seemed workable was tried. A few practices seemed to work well in some areas and later developed the semblance of policy. Even these were later unevenly applied, depending on the circumstances. These issues will become clearer as we examine colonial administrative practices of the various European powers.

Early British Colonial Administration—The Legislative Councils

British administrative systems for governing her colonies in Africa varied. At one end of the spectrum involved the white settler colonies of Northern and Southern Rhodesia, Kenya and Nyasaland, influenced by the practice in South Africa, and the older colonial enclaves like the coastal segments of what became the colonies of Sierra Leone, the Gold Coast and Nigeria. In the white settler territories, the British allowed for administrative units called Legislative Councils. Northern and Southern Rhodesia were initially ruled on behalf of Britain by Rhodes' British South Africa Company (BSAC). Northern Rhodesia was in fact ruled by the British settlers who flocked there on the encouragement of the British government which reserved extensive fertile land for white settlers. It was not until 1923 that Southern Rhodesia (1929 for Northern Rhodesia) was finally brought under direct British administration.

The Legislative Councils in these white settler territories were meant only for the white settlers who could pass laws that were detrimental to the Africans, but served to entrench white positions in these colonies. The Legislative Councils had been created by the BSAC and when the British government took over from that company, the system continued with the white settlers pressing for more control. The British government agreed in 1945 to give the four thousand whites in Northern Rhodesia control in the Legislative Council over the destiny of the one million blacks. The Legislative Councils in the white settler territories were in no way democratic institutions as they were instruments for the white minority to elect only their own kind to dominate the black majority with the support of the British government.

Similar direct administration involving Legislative Councils were set up in Egypt. The situation in Egypt and the Sudan involved British administration in cooperation with the Turkish ruler, since Egypt was still technically a province of Turkey. In practice, the British disregarded the Turkish ruler's authority and ruled Egypt as a British colony. The Legislative Council and Assembly, set up to ensure participation of the Egyptians, were all but disregarded. Egyptians filled junior positions as in other British colonies. The Sudan, regarded as a unit under both Egyptian and British control, was ruled in much similar ways. Supposed to be a joint British and Egyptian administration, the British completely ignored Egyptian participation, arguing that Egyptians were corrupt and that under the rule of Turkey and Egypt in the nineteenth century, the Sudan had been maltreated.

The Legislative Councils in the non-white settler colonies like Sierra Leone, Nigeria, Nyasaland, were equally not meant to serve African interests. They were largely based on representatives appointed by the British governor. The council served only a small segment of the administration of these territories, the larger areas being ruled by different methods. The councils did not really legislate; they only advised the governor who was free to reject their advice, which he often did. Some semblance of election of local African representatives into these Legislative Councils was attempted on one or two occasions, but it was only for a couple of members to the council, the rest being usually British officials in the colony.

Administration of Non-Settler Populations

Outside the colonial capitals, the British initially felt their way. Territories were broken down into districts, within which were smaller units called chiefdoms. Some of these chiefdoms conformed to pre-colonial political units, but the majority did not. Many pre-colonial political units, too large to serve the administrative interests of the British, were broken up into smaller chiefdom units. That way, they would be too small to organize threatening rebellion to British rule. The term 'paramount chief' was introduced by the

British, referring to the local heads of these chiefdoms. Some paramount chiefs were former rulers or descended from ruling families. For others, their only claim to ruling was their agility to do the bidding of the British.

The major transition was to get paramount chiefs to transfer allegiance from pre-colonial principles of legitimacy to the British. Where formerly they had depended on the consent of their people based on prestige derived from leadership in war, ritual, oratory and the like, the British now made it clear that their positions depended on their new colonial masters. Those who showed that they understood this stayed in their positions. The others were summarily removed and replaced.

This new dispensation made paramount chiefs less dependent on their people and consequently more able to exploit them. Problems were to arise as paramount chiefs began to enrich themselves at the expense of their people. As long as they could retain the support of the British, this was fine. It only broke down in some areas when the people revolted. The British too became increasingly dependent on these 'new' African rulers which only strengthened the powers of paramount chiefs.

Indirect Rule

The most successful and vaunted pattern of British administration of her African colonies has been described as indirect rule. It involved a policy of governing African colonies where possible by using their own local institutions and systems of rule.

The emergence of this system is usually credited to Frederick Lugard who was made High Commissioner for the Protectorate of Northern Nigeria in 1900 after seeing service in Nyasaland and Uganda. But as we have mentioned earlier, the practice of using local figures, now called paramount chiefs, with some claim to hereditary rule, had started in many areas of British colonial rule before 1900. It was virtually impossible for the British to import large numbers of British personnel to these African colonies for administration. The costs would have been prohibitive and in any case British people did not want to serve in most areas of British Africa where they had learnt one could quickly die of malaria from mosquito bites. And in any case, the British, like the other colonial rulers, had come to Africa to gain material benefit, by extracting commodities, so they wanted to spend as little time, money and attention to administration as possible. Thus a system of using local rulers and to some degree local customs which had started in British West African colonies in Nigeria, the Gold Coast and Sierra Leone, seemed appropriate.

It was Lugard however who seized the opportunity of making this into a philosophy and giving it a more clearly defined focus. He even wrote a book about this, which he called *The Dual Mandate in Tropical Africa*, and became very famous among the European powers on this issue. The 'dual mandate' according to Lugard, was that at the same time as deriving material benefit from the African colonies, the colonial ruler had an obligation to uplift the Africans and by this he meant taking some British values to them.

Lugard found an efficient system of administration among the *emirates* (Muslim states ruled by an *emir*) in the heavily populated region of what became Northern Nigeria. Here the emirs had systems for the administration of justice, collection of taxes, organization of public works and others. Lacking British personnel, Lugard developed a positive attitude towards using this system in the emirates. The defeated emirs, once assured that Lugard intended to 'respect' their positions and succession and allow them to continue collecting taxes, readily cooperated. Lugard put his own stamp on the system in the emirates by setting up higher protectorate courts as courts of Appeal from the emir's courts. He also got the emirs, now called chiefs, to pay a fourth of the taxes collected to the colonial government. Of the rest, another portion was paid into what Lugard called Native Treasuries. These Treasuries also received fees and fines from the judicial processes. From the treasuries, salaries were paid to local government officials. All of this was labeled a system of 'Native Administration.'

All of this would be supervised by a British official who was the ultimate power in the chiefdom. This system worked well in the centralized government found among the Hausa and Fulani peoples of northern Nigeria. Lugard became so righteous about the success of using local institutions in the indirect rule system that he kept all Christian missionary influence from northern Nigeria while he was there, for fear that they could adversely influence a system based on Islamic principles that had become his success. This was to have adverse consequences for Nigeria later on, for colonial rule ultimately depended on a westernized educated elite and this education was largely brought by Christian missionaries. Insulating northern Nigeria from western education while the south of Nigeria received this meant that much later, after the glare of indirect rule had died down, people from the south began to assume administrative positions in northern Nigeria in numbers large enough to create dissatisfaction among the northerners. This was a contributory factor to the Nigerian civil war of 1967.

But at the beginning of the twentieth century, Native Administration based on indirect rule was hailed as a success by the British who began using a similar system to modify administration in a number of colonies. Native Administration was introduced in the Gold Coast among the Fante and Asante peoples starting after 1931, in Sierra Leone from 1939 and in the Gambia Protectorate after 1933.

The implementation of indirect rule outside of Northern Nigeria did not meet with equal success. This was more evident in southern Nigeria in the wake of Lugard's indirect rule. After the initial success in the north, Lugard left Nigeria in 1906 to return in 1912 as Governor of both southern and northern Nigeria. Lugard then tried to implement his system in southern Nigeria. The two dominant groups in southern Nigeria are the Yoruba and Igbo. The Yoruba had centralized political system headed by rulers called *oba*. The *oba's* powers were however hedged in by councils, laws and religious beliefs. The conversion of the *oba* into a paramount chief now dependent on the British for his authority, removed these checks on the *oba's* power and thereby increased his power. *Obas* now tended to become overbearing and their people no longer had any control over them, a situation similar to paramount chiefs in other areas of the British Empire. There was in fact a rebellion in 1918 among one Yoruba group, the Egba, against Lugard's methods of direct taxation, which had worked well in northern Nigeria, but were totally alien to the Egba.

The Igbo of eastern Nigeria had been organized in smaller political units. There were consequently no traditional rulers who wielded wider authority to be made paramount chiefs. The British had initially appointed some individuals as chiefs and certified them with warrants, so that they came to be called 'warrant chiefs.' They had been responsible for trying minor cases and supervising government construction by providing free labor.

When Lugard took control of all of this area he quickly promoted some of these warrant chiefs to become paramount chiefs. These Igbo paramount chiefs had no relationship to any form of authority in the past with the Igbo people. They were therefore not respected which made their work more difficult. After Lugard left Nigeria, enough hostility had been generated towards these colonial chiefs that it burst out into rebellion led by the powerful market women in the town of Aba. This movement against these agents of colonial rule came to be known as the *ogu omuwanyi* (women's war). Colonial forces were called in and many women were shot to death before the rebellion ended.

French Colonial Administration

In some ways like the British, French colonial administration did not follow a consistent pattern. We have to remember that such administration in Africa had started well before the partition of Africa. The French had established an outpost in the coastal area of Senegal before the nineteenth century. This gradually expanded into an area with political divisions into four communes—Dakar, Gorée, Rufisque and St. Louis. Communes were political divisions existent in France itself and the French tended in this earlier colonial period to rule their colonies after a pattern that operated in France. It was a similar situation in Algeria which had become a French colony since 1830. The situation in Algeria involved a large body of French settlers who moved there over the years. They were referred to as the *colons* and they became a privileged minority as in South Africa.

In both Algeria and Senegal, those who were regarded as citizens could vote their own representatives (Deputies, they were called) into the French Assembly or parliament. The French then regarded their colonies as an extension of France itself—*France d'outre mer* (overseas France). In Algeria however, only the colons were French citizens and so the deputies in the French Assembly represented the interest of the colons which meant alienation of the best lands and exploitation of the labor of the Arab and Berber subjects.

In the four communes of Senegal, Africans acquired French citizenship following a policy of assimilation. By this policy, the French ruled out any attachment to African culture which they regarded as primitive and barbarous. All Africans who disregarded their culture and acquired French culture and education and thus a certain level of income, could become French citizens and thus be eligible to vote for deputies to the French Assembly. The entrenched Islamic element in the culture of the Africans in the four communes was the most difficult to handle so the French made a concession here, recognizing Muslim courts in the four communes. The first of these was opened in St. Louis in 1848. Thus Africans in the four communes could qualify as French citizens but still be governed by Islamic law in matters like marriage, inheritance and wills. Apart from the Deputies to the French Assembly, the four communes also had their own local councils, the *Conseil-Général du Senegal* by 1879.

The French virtually abandoned this policy of assimilation after acquiring a large African empire by the end of the nineteenth century. The French declared Tunisia and Morocco as protectorates, in a fashion similar to the

British, and proceeded to set up an administration using the indigenous Islamic authorities in both colonies. Similar indigenous authorities were initially used by the French in isolated areas like among the Mossi in Upper Volta. In the rest of French West Africa (AOF) where the French took over a continuous geographical area stretching across the western Sudan, each colony was administered by a lieutenant-governor, a French official who answered to a Governor-General in Senegal. Another section of French colonies in central Africa involving the colonies of Gabon, Congo (Brazzaville), and Ubanghi-Chari (Central African Republic), was referred to as French Equatorial Africa (AEF). Each territory was further broken down into *cercles* under a *commandant* who was a French officer. *Cercles* were sub-divided into *cantons*, each under a *chef de canton* (canton chiefs).

In the appointment of canton chiefs, the French paid very little regard to any traditional principles that had existed before French rule. Their major concern was to prevent any coalition of interests against France. Their policy was thus one of 'the progressive suppression of the great chiefs and the parceling out of their authority.' This policy was most noticeable in Senegal outside the four communes, and in Guinea. In the latter, the French ignored the agreement they had made to respect the *Imam*, the traditional ruler of the Futa Jalon area. The ruling *Imam*, Bademba, was deposed in 1879 and a French nominee put in his place. Soon therefore the *imamate*, the indigenous political unit in Futa Jalon, was broken up into three provinces. By 1912, the *Imams* were being regarded as canton chiefs. These canton chiefs therefore depended on the French for their positions. Their judicial functions were greatly restricted. They were basically collectors of taxes that went entirely to the French. Their ability to carry out this task effectively came to define their authority.

Thus by the twentieth century, the French came to de-emphasize the assimilation policy which would have been too costly to implement over the entire French African colonies. The restrictions for qualification were in fact so severe that many could not qualify. By 1939, after over forty years of French rule, only some five hundred Africans outside the four communes had acquired French citizenship.

Aside from disregarding traditional authority in the appointment of canton chiefs, the French even began to show more serious concern about the potential for Islamic leaders assuming leadership of discontent against French rule. Thus there was a movement to restrict Islamic leadership and influence even in the four communes. The French soon prohibited the use of Arabic, the language of Islam, in the courts in the four communes and, by 1911, its use in official correspondence. No Muslim courts could be set up outside the four communes. Policy was developed to limit the number of traditional Islamic schools being set up in Senegal.

Thus a more pro-French, anti-traditional administration was progressively developed by the French. It was a very centralized system following the pattern in France itself. This was buttressed by the education thinly provided at a higher level at the École Normale William Ponty in Dakar. There the few privileged Africans from all the colonies met and, when qualified, could be deployed often away from their territories of origin.

French administration was initially very harsh with a heavy dependence on forced labor organized by the administration. The code of law called the *indigénat* was applied since 1887. This was a system of arbitrary punishment without trial of people declared as criminals. This was administered by white officials at the level of commandant and above. It severely undermined the judicial authority of the chiefs. A system of head tax was imposed, supplemented by a tax in labor called *prestation*, which could be redeemed with cash. All males eighteen to fifty years of age had to fulfil *prestation* for ten days in the year. This rate was higher, up to fifteen days in AEF. Laws for the recruitment of forced labor were amended by 1921, but they did little to alter the situation. Forced labor in AEF was more rampant and it was controlled by the colonial administration. People forcefully drafted to work were not even provided with food. They had to be fed by the local community within walking distance of their place of work.

When the French embarked on the construction of a railway from Congo to Océan, hundreds of thousands of workers were coerced into the construction at very low wages. The brutal conditions of work took a heavy toll on the population. It is estimated that more than twenty thousand lives were lost before 1928 in the construction of this railway. The Fang population of the region was reduced by this exercise from 140,000 to 65,000 by 1933. People were also forced to grow crops like cotton, even foodstuff like cassava during the First World War. All of these commodities, even the foodstuff, were exported and the growers paid very little for their labor or the commodities. In Gabon, only a quarter of the foodstuff in enforced production was not exported and therefore left for local consumption. Up to 1919, these farm communities were paid in kind for these goods, valued very low by the colonial administration, and they were heavily taxed from the meager proceeds. These demands led to considerable labor migration from poorer colonies like Upper Volta and Niger to plantation colonies like Ivory Coast and the Gold Coast where people could sell their labor for better wages to pay the taxes.

Portuguese Colonial Administration

The Portuguese held colonies in Mozambique, Angola and the tiny enclave of Guinea Bissau and the Cape Verde Islands in West Africa. Portugal was a poorer country in Europe; and consequently depended more heavily on her colonies. In this part of middle Africa where Portuguese, Belgian (in the Congo) and French colonies bordered each other, colonial practices were very similar.

One dominant feature was the government of these territories by companies given a charter by the Portuguese government. The largely British owned Niasa Company ruled northern Mozambique while the southern area was dominated by the Mozambique Company. Other companies received contracts for administration and exploitation of various parts of the colonies. This situation of company rule was only amended in 1930 when the Portuguese government took over.

These companies were only interested in exploiting minerals and the labor of the people living there. The hiring out of labor from Angola to the South African mines and to the cocoa plantations of Sao Tome became the chief economic activity in these colonies. A South African company recruiting labor for mining in the Transvaal entered into agreement with the colonial government in Mozambique to provide this labor. It is estimated that between 1913 and 1930, at least 50,000 laborers were sent to South Africa from Mozambique by this arrangement. Out of the total of some 900,000 for that period, about 35,000 died from the hardship endured in the process. Labor was also coerced through the demands of high taxation. Taxation in the colonial period was highest in the Portuguese colonies, equivalent to three months labor annually. As taxation was paid in labor, this provided a ready means of forcing people into unpaid labor for extended periods.

When the Portuguese hit on successfully growing cocoa in the islands of Sao Tome and Principe about the turn of the century, they began shipping close to four thousand people each year from Angola. These were forced labor victims but their recruitment was labeled as free labor. Many lost their lives as they sometimes rebelled on board the ships which transported them in conditions identical to those of the middle passage in the Atlantic slave trade. Virtual slavery returned to the Portuguese colonies until this forced the reaction of the other European countries. Conventions passed by the League of Nations as late as 1930 against Portugal's disguised slave labor were rejected by Portugal. In 1947, a Portuguese who represented Angola in the Portuguese parliament reported that two million Africans had been transported from the Portuguese colonies in the forced labor migration pattern. Portugal only slowly abandoned the worst of these practices as international pressure piled up.

Harsh conditions of forced labor provoked repeated rebellions in this part of Portuguese Africa. In the Barue kingdom in Mozambique, which had rebelled against the Portuguese in 1904, thousands of African males were being conscripted into forced labor under brutal conditions. The Portuguese were building a road through the Barue kingdom during the First World War. Many were also being conscripted into the colonial army. The combined pressure of this conscription prompted a rebellion in 1917 led by an individual named Nongwe-Nongwe. He built up a strong alliance among different groups spreading into Rhodesia. The rebellion was initially successful but the Portuguese later succeeded in allying with another African group, the Ngoni, to put down the rebellion.

Forced labor, provided by the Portuguese regulation of 1899, was also used for cultivation. There was compulsory cultivation of crops like groundnuts in Guinea Bissau, cotton in Mozambique, and the enforced collection of rubber in Angola before 1912 when rubber growing wild was exhausted. Commodities so obtained had to be sold to the European companies at extremely low prices determined by the companies.

Forced labor aside, those not recruited experienced equally brutal treatment at the hands of ill-trained and educated colonial officials. Pass laws were instituted to control the population and keep them pinned down to where they were located. In spite of all of this, massive migration took place from the Portuguese colonies to neighboring areas. From Mozambique and Angola, there was constant migration to British colonies like Nyasaland and the Rhodesias where conditions were more humane. Similar migrations occurred from Guinea Bissau to the neighboring French territories, particularly in Senegal.

Belgian Colonial Administration

No other colonial rule in Africa was marked with more atrocities than that of the Belgians. Belgium ruled the large colony of the Congo and after the First World War, inherited the tiny neighboring colonies of Rwanda and Burundi from Germany, as the defeated Germany lost all of her colonies in Africa. As mentioned earlier, the Belgian colony of the Congo was initially colonized by Leopold, King of Belgium as a private estate and named the

Congo Free State. It was not until 1908, after over thirty years of personal rule, that the Congo was placed under the Belgian government.

Both Leopold and after him the Belgian government, ruled large segments of the Congo through concession companies like the Katanga company of Union Minière which had exclusive mineral rights in one area. The only concern of the administration here was to provide labor for mining and forced cultivation. The initial concern, however, was for rubber cultivation to support industry in Europe, especially after the development of the motorcar. In both the Congo and neighboring Angola, rubber became the king in the 1890s and 1900s. Rubber exports from the Congo rose from two tons in 1891 to 6,000 tons in 1901.

Leopold declared as vacant all land not visibly utilized by the people of the Congo. All such 'vacant' land belonged to the government. This of course meant hardship to the people since by a bush fallow system of shifting cultivation, not all land was immediately used. Seizing such land seemingly idle meant destroying the agricultural system of the populace.

Rubber production became the source of the wildest abominations in the Congo Free State. Leopold's and other company officials used armies of renegades to force the people to collect rubber. Quotas were given to villages which, if not fulfilled, meant the destruction of villages, shooting of inhabitants and frequent cutting off of limbs, breasts and ears of the people. One European visitor reported a supervisor counting the number of hacked limbs to ensure that bullets supplied had not been wasted. There was a spate of rebellions in this early period, put down with much brutality by these new Congo rulers. Many people migrated to neighboring French Congo, losing all their land and resources. Some who returned at night to collect some goods, were shot on sight. As rebellions rose and the price of rubber fell, Leopold, who had become very wealthy from Congo Free State resources, was pressured to hand over control of the Congo to the Belgian government. This ended some of the worst abuses, though it did not end the influence and control of the private companies. In 1911, in fact, the English firm of Lever Brothers was granted monopoly of palm products in a huge area of the Congo.

In the process of exploiting rubber, Leopold gave concession to a company to build a railway between the towns of Matadi and Kinshasa. Begun in 1899, work on this railway only added to the misery of the Congo people as many were put to work under appalling conditions. Even so, labor for the railway was inadequate and contract labor was imported from British colonies in Sierra Leone and Nigeria, even from China, to meet the shortfall.

But these labor contracts were disguised slavery and many fled from their contract before it was over. It is estimated that under Leopold, the population of the Congo Free State "is said to have declined from 20 or 30 million to eight million."

At the end of the rubber boom, a consistent forced labor policy was pursued to support the mines of Katanga and enforced cultivation of cotton and rice that was exported. Labor was exported from Rwanda to Katanga in huge numbers. The harsh conditions of labor and meaningless wages were attended by natural calamities like the great famine in Rwanda in 1928/9. Many migrated to neighboring countries like Uganda. This caused shortage of labor in the mines and railways and the colonial authorities began to pay some attention after 1928 to labor regulations to ameliorate the harsh conditions. But labor recruitment with unsavory practices continued. In 1926, the Congo Free State administration delegated to the Bourse du Travail du Katanga, a private agency, its powers of recruitment of labor. Similar recruitment awards were made to other companies.

The impact of all of these policies was devastating on the population. Colonial administration was in this context utterly callous in its disregard for the basic humanity of the colonial peoples or for any form of orderly government.

Conclusion

As mentioned earlier, there was much similarity in policies and cooperation between the colonial powers in Central and southern Africa where British, French, Portuguese and at the initial phase German colonies, had common borders. Primarily through the German East Africa Company, the Germans too had ruled Tanganyika, Rwanda and Burundi in this region, but also her colonies in South West Africa, Cameroons and Togo in West Africa. Each of these colonial rulers in this region of central Africa kept a sizable para-military force used to recruit labor, collect taxes and generally to take care of threats to colonial authority. Some of the highest taxes and the most brutal methods of tax collection were employed by the Germans, French, Portuguese and the Congo Free State administration in this general area of Central Africa. There was no intention to set up any costly administration so the local chiefs were used, more as hostages, to get access to the population, than as administrators. The ruthless armed forces were quick to burn villages, shoot or maim individuals at the slightest suspicion of resistance or failure to comply with harsh commands for labor or resources.

These cruel policies led to frequent rebellions in the early colonial period against all of these colonial rulers. The Chagga people fought the German tax collectors in 1900. In Angola repeated clashes were followed by larger protests like the 1902 Bailundu rising on the Bihe Plateau. The Nandi also rebelled against the British twice in 1902 and 1905. Finally many different ethnic groups, some formerly hostile to each other, got together and led a widespread rebellion against the Congo Free State government in 1904, while another such uproar flared up in 1905 in the Lulonga District. 145 of the agents of the rubber trading company were killed. But all of these rebellions were eventually quelled with much bloodshed.

These atrocities were less evident in British West Africa and the Senegal area ruled by the French. The description of colonial rule in these areas therefore does not represent a general picture of patterns of colonial rule in Africa. We will later discuss changes in colonial rule particularly in the period after the Second World War.

Questions

1. Present a picture of the variety of British colonial administrative patterns in Africa before the Second World War.
2. In what ways did colonial administrative practices affect labor recruitment in the colonies in Africa?

Chapter IV

ॐ

The Colonial Economy

There are certain factors common to the activities of all the colonial powers in Africa. Firstly, colonial powers came to Africa to exploit the resources of the land. Consideration of the interest of the African peoples was at best minimal, and this often became evident if it could serve the interest of exploitation. At worst, these interests were non-existent.

It also needs to be pointed out that there was extensive and continuing collusion between the colonial interests in the exploitation of the African colonies. Private companies worked hand in hand with the colonial governments both to impose and execute regulations beneficial either to white settler communities or the interests of European capital and governments.

In the process of colonial economic exploitation, certain residual benefits fell to the Africans. But these were largely unintended. One of the most pronounced benefit was the drawing of African countries very forcefully into the global capitalist system.

Particularly in the initial period, the first couple of decades, one of the major concerns of the European imperialists was that of moving Africans from their own economic systems and interests to working in the interest of European capital. Africans were mostly peasant farmers producing largely for their own consumption. They did not, at the start of colonial rule, show any significant interest in leaving their own economic activity to work for

European interests. They therefore had to be coerced by a variety of methods. The main elements used for this coercion were high taxation, land alienation and forced labor. The attraction of European imported goods also played a part in the process of getting Africans hooked to working in the interest of Europeans. Let us look at these factors in turn.

Taxation

One of the first instruments of domination in the African colonies was taxation. All European colonies imposed taxation and increased these as they deemed it useful to drive Africans out of their self-employed agricultural systems. To pay these high taxes, Africans would be forced to sell their labor as the crops they grew, undervalued by the Europeans, were inadequate to pay the taxes. The governor of Kenya summed this up neatly in 1913 thus:

> We consider that taxation is the only possible method of compelling the native to leave his reserve for the purpose of seeking work.... It is on this that the supply of labour and the price of labour depend. To raise the rate of wages would not increase, but would diminish the supply of labor.

Wages paid were usually very low; a month's wages were often only slightly higher than the quantum of tax.

Taxes were levied in a variety of ways. The British levied primarily a house tax and also a head tax on any adult individual in the colonies. In the French, Portuguese and Congo Free State areas, taxes were often payable in labor, so that it became simply a means of coercing labor. In the Portuguese colonies, the head tax was the \equivalent officially of three month's labor a year. In the Belgian Congo after 1916, Africans began to receive cash payments for work instead of payment in kind. What followed was a rapid increase in the rate of the head tax that could not keep pace with wages, particularly in the period between the two world wars when a great depression set in. Some of these peasants in the Belgian Congo who grew compulsory crops like cotton, received wages of 165 to 170 Belgian Francs per year and by the early 1930s had to pay tax at 122 Belgian francs per annum. In the French colony of Ubanghi-Chari, another example, peasants earned in the same period wages between 9.2 and 40 French francs while they had to pay taxes at 11 French francs. The peasants usually experienced only an increase in the tax burden. For example, between 1929 and 1934, the tax increased forty-three percent in AEF, with no corresponding increase in wages.

These examples given above were in some of the worst areas, but there is clearly no doubt that high taxation coupled with low wages and under valuation of the food crops Africans produced contributed significantly in forcing Africans from their basic food producing economies into wage labor for European interests.

Forced Labor

Taxation, as explained, was often tied up with labor. High taxation always went with low wages for labor. When wages were low, people would be disinclined to sell their labor. The need for labor therefore had to be met partly by forcing Africans to work for European interests. Again, all European colonialists used forced labor though it was radically worse in certain colonies than in others.

Forced labor took different forms. It sometimes meant compulsory cultivation of crops the Europeans wanted like cotton in Ubanghi-Chari, Tanganyika and Uganda, or groundnuts in Senegal. In other instances, it meant quota recruitment by colonial authorities from settlements for public works and this was largely unpaid or paid with rations or extremely low wages. Disguised forced labor also meant keeping wages very low while alienating the fertile land so that Africans could not farm but would be forced to work for low wages from European plantations or mines.

Forced labor was harsher in some colonies than in others. In the British West African colonies, it largely meant extremely low wages for carriers and rail workers at the start of the colonial period. It was worse in the British settler colonies of Kenya, the Rhodesias and Nyasaland. Here white settler immigrants from South Africa and Britain, meant a dominant minority who could influence colonial laws on land and labor to their own benefit. In Kenya, for example, the *kipande*, a pass system similar to that in South Africa, was introduced in 1920. Adult males had to carry the *kipande* and if they lost it, were subject to fines or imprisonment for three months. The *kipande* carried information on time worked, nature of work and wages; it was a criminal offence for Africans to abandon their employment. In Southern Rhodesia where Europeans engaged more predominantly in farming, starvation wages were paid to the Africans.

We mentioned in the previous chapter the official exploitation of labor in the Portuguese, French colonies and the Belgian Congo. It is enough to add here that the Portuguese had pass laws to regulate labor in Angola and Mozambique similar to those in Kenya. One form of the coercion of labor in the beginning of the colonial period was in the use of quota production to acquire commodities that grew in forested areas and only needed collection. The chief of this was rubber. Both in the Congo Free State, in the Portuguese colony of Angola and French colony of Guinea, quotas were imposed on villages for the delivery of wild rubber. We have discussed the results of failure to meet such quotas in the Belgian Congo. So ridiculous were these quotas that in the French Guinea the peasants responded by adulterating the latex with pebbles that were undiscoverable when the latex gelled. This gave the rubber more weight to meet the quotas until the French discovered this trick.

Land Alienation

The use of land as a weapon to free Africans to sell their labor was more common in the British colonies in Central and East Africa where there were white settlers. Large portions of the most fertile land were reserved by the colonial government to encourage white settlers to emigrate to these colonies. In Southern Rhodesia, the BSAC promised 6,000 acres of land to each of the white settlers from South Africa who joined their forces to defeat the Ndebele in 1892.

In Kenya some 2,000 hectares of land had been taken over by Europeans by 1903. This rose to 260,000 by 1914 and to about 2,740,000 by 1930. The British Lord Delamere alone 'owned' 400,000 hectares. Up to 1915, the land was leased to these British settlers for ninety-nine years by the Crown Land Ordinance. Thereafter the leases were extended by law to 999 years and the minimal 'rent' paid to the British government on the land was further reduced.

In 1904 and again in 1911, the Maasai of Kenya were twice expropriated from their land and herded into 'Native Reserves.' This meant movement from fertile land to overcrowded, often barren land on which the Africans could not profitably farm. In Southern Rhodesia, the European settlers had grabbed 7,700,000 hectares of land by 1911. This had risen to 12.5 million by 1925. By the latter year, Africans had only been able to purchase only 18,000 hectares outside the Native Reserves. All of these land alienation policies were based on laws passed by the colonial government either to confirm existing land claims by Europeans or to appropriate new land.

British land alienation policies were weaker in West Africa because that area did not attract European settlers due to its more hostile climate. In addition, the small African elite from the earlier colonial enclaves in Lagos,

Nigeria, the Gold Coast and Sierra Leone was vocal in protesting such policies. All the colonial rulers felt free to and often arbitrarily reserved territory for mining, forest reserves and the like.

By these methods African labor was progressively proleterianized. This was helped along by European goods which, as the colonial period wore on, Africans became attached to and would therefore sell labor to acquire such goods.

Colonial Agricultural Production Patterns

Agriculture remained the dominant mode of extraction in most of these colonies. This was primarily agriculture for export, even when compulsory production was providing food crop commodities.

Agricultural products exported from these colonies were generally determined by demands in Europe. By the late nineteenth century, the demand was still based on fats and oils to lubricate machinery, so that palm oil products were popular. With the development of the internal combustion engine and thus the automobile, there was a great need for rubber for tires and a variety of other related uses. This ushered in a rubber boom which absorbed the energies of colonial rulers in colonies like the Congo Free State, Angola, Sierra Leone, Guinea where rubber grew wild and only needed collection. The aggregation of naturally growing rubber and palm products dominated the colonial economies particularly in these named colonies in the early colonial period.

The idea of developing plantation economies however gained momentum. This idea related to crops to be grown for sale, often referred to as cash crops. A variety of such crops were tried with varying degrees of success. One of the most prominent was cotton, intended to support manufacturing in Europe. Cotton plantations were started with compulsory cultivation particularly in Egypt, Uganda, Tanganyika, Ubanghi-Chari, Belgian Congo and Nyasaland. Enforced growing of cotton in plantations run by the state were organized in Belgian, French and German colonies, while in others companies were given purchasing monopolies. Colonial government subsidies were provided in AOF and seeds distributed with technical instructions. The Portuguese relied only on local initiatives which failed miserably as Africans had no experience with that pattern of cotton plantations.

Other cash crops introduced in similar ways with greater success were coffee and cocoa. Coffee plantations based on enforced labor were introduced in French, Belgian and Portuguese colonies. In Rwanda-Urundi each chief or sub-chief was obliged to cultivate half a hectare when this started in 1925. Coffee and cocoa production was also introduced in some British colonies. In white settler colonies of Kenya and the Rhodesias, every attempt was made to keep the production of whatever turned out to be a lucrative crop in the hands of white settlers. In Kenya, for example, Africans were forbidden to grow coffee, the most profitable crop. Only the success of the Mau Mau movement ended this. Prices of crops produced by Africans were kept artificially low by buying organizations set up by the colonial governments.

In British colonies where there were no white settlers, Africans organized the production of especially cocoa and coffee on a large scale. Assistance provided by the colonial government here was minimal, with woefully ignorant white extension workers. But Africans thrived here nonetheless. In fact cocoa growing was introduced into the Gold Coast towards the end of the nineteenth century by an indigenous contract laborer named Tetteh Quasi who was returning from Fernando Po at the end of his contract. Mostly by the farmers' own efforts, the Gold Coast became a leading world cocoa producer, exporting forty percent of the world output by 1934.

One long term result of the concentration on one specific crop which grew well in one colony was the development of mono crop economies in certain colonies. This trait was carried over into the post-colonial era as newly independent countries inherited and continued the economic systems which had taken root under colonialism. Thus Senegal became known for groundnut and Ghana for cocoa. Liberia, though not a colony, was dominated by United States influence in this same period. Rubber plantations were started by Harvey Firestone in Liberia early in the twentieth century and Liberia came to depend significantly on this crop.

In all of this agricultural scramble, little attention was given to food crop production and Africans continued to produce food crops by their own traditional methods. Where they succeeded and began to gain a strong market for this, as with maize production in the Rhodesias, the white settlers were quick to exploit this and debase the prices for these products by controlled organizations.

In some French territories and the Belgian Congo, food crops consumed locally were produced by compulsory labor for export. But what most adversely affected the population was the enforced commandering of foodstuff particularly during the First World War and the extremely high taxation particularly in the French colonies that forced people to sell off their goods and food supply. If they fled to another place, the collective payment system in the French territories meant that those left behind had to pay taxes for the departed.

Mining

Colonial exploration for raw materials led to prospecting for minerals which were found in varying quantities in certain colonies—copper in the Belgian Congo and Northern Rhodesia, iron ore in Liberia and Sierra Leone, tin in Nigeria, gold in the Gold Coast, diamonds in Sierra Leone and so on.

Mining represented one of the areas of the greatest capital expenditure of the colonial rulers. though much of this was evident in the white settler colonies. Most railways were directed to areas of mining. Concessions for mining were given on extremely generous leases to European concerns to mine these minerals. In the diamond mines of Sierra Leone for example, a ninety-nine year lease was awarded to the Sierra Leone Selection Trust, a subsidiary of the De Beers conglomerate, to mine diamonds anywhere in Sierra Leone. Even for the mining of minerals that were not particularly profitable, free labor used initially made them viable. In the tin mining in Nigeria, for example, thousands of people from neighboring French Niger, fleeing famine and high taxation there, formed a large pool of labor, making it possible for the tin mining concessionaries to further lower the already low wages paid to the miners.

Mining provided jobs and wages, though low, were generally better than in agriculture. In certain areas, mining led to dramatic social change, particularly the growth of urban centers that had previously been tiny villages. The growth of the town of Koidu in the diamond mines in Sierra Leone is one example. From a small village of ninety-six people in 1927, Koidu became a town of nearly 12,000 by 1963.

One of the areas of greatest urbanization due to mining was the area called the Copperbelt in northern Rhodesia. New methods of mining sulphide ores led to a boom in copper mining by large capitalist companies. White migration, particularly from South Africa, increased. These whites entrenched their position with increased numbers and with the assistance of the colonial government that seized land to hold for white immigrants. The mining also led to the relatively increased prosperity of what became the copperbelt towns. These were increasingly urbanized settlements that sprang up around the mines as it became necessary for African workers to stay close by rather than commute from distant settlements. In addition, some

Africans began receiving increased wages for semi-skilled jobs since there were not enough whites to fill such positions.

It became possible for these relatively prosperous Africans to give their children better education. They became more familiar with the values of the westernized urban centers and conscious of their own rights, in an atmosphere of racism by the white settlers who controlled the economy and the government. These workers were thereby strengthened to protest these elements in more formal ways and thus formed the vanguard of an incipient nationalism.

Mining also encouraged the formation of trade unions that became a major source of protest in the colonial period. Although such unions were largely forbidden by the colonial rulers, determined workers insisted on forming them to bargain for better working conditions or to protest. It was easier for Africans to form such unions in the white settler colonies since the example of white worker unions, which were permitted, was a strong incentive for the setting up of African trade unions.

Railways

Railways represented an important area of capital expenditure in the colonial period. Since road systems were poor and river transport was unreliable, early construction of railways was evident, particularly necessary to move bulk goods and people in large numbers. While most rail lines were within single colonies, some connected more than one colony, like the Congo-Ocean railway which linked Ubanghi-Chari (Central African Republic) and the French Congo (Brazzaville).

Railways were primarily intended to provide ready access to areas for the extraction of certain commodities. The Accra to Kumasi railway in the Cold Coast was to access cocoa producing areas. The Freetown to Pendembu line in Sierra Leone was directed to an area rich in palm products. The Benguela railway in Angola was directed to the copper mines of Katanga, while the Kenya-Uganda Railway opened up cotton growing in Uganda.

The financing of these railways was not always simply a matter of investment by the colonial rulers. The use of forced labor for construction was rampant particularly in the French, Belgian, German and Portuguese colonies. Meager rations were provided for the workers in some instances. In the construction of the Congo-Ocean railway, the inhabitants were expected to provide food for the workers if the path of construction was within a day's walk from any existing settlement. Since this work, for extended hours in each day, withdrew significant labor from farming for food supply, famine resulted as families were not provided for. It is estimated that such famine probably reduced the Fang population of the Congo area by half in the mid 1920s. This made the weakened peoples fall prey to epidemics of smallpox and Spanish influenza, further decimating the population. We have already mentioned the impact of this development in the Congo-Ocean railway.

In many other territories labor was paid for with extremely low wages. The Conakry to Kankan railway in French Guinea was constructed with budgetary surplus from the heavy taxation levied on the peoples. The twelve million French francs loaned by the French government to build the railway were repaid with this surplus. Again, this was built with virtually free labor, meager rations and no wages being given the laborers.

Apart from their intended use, railways had other significant benefits for the colonial rulers. Railways provided a facility for improving communication with areas where the colonial authorities had had difficulty in bringing about effective administration—indeed to areas they sometimes hardly knew up to a decade after the start of colonial rule in such colonies. Railways spurred trade between the colonial capitals and the interior, encouraging the construction of feeder roads by the local peoples, linking settlements a distance away with the railway. Since railways could move bulk goods, they became a vehicle for the rapid penetration of western goods into the interior of most African colonies. Along with these were also transported western values, providing for Africans a strong attraction to the colonial economies. This was sometimes harmful for local industries, as for example the relative flooding of the interior markets with western clothing dealt a harmful blow to the indigenous production of cloth.

For the inhabitants, railways provided access to better incomes for enterprising peoples wherever the railways led. But the rail also made movements in and out of hitherto secluded communities more possible, facilitating the easy exit for criminals and entrance for western culture that condemned African values.

Railways were also less beneficial than they could have been to the colonial peoples. Because of the main reason for their construction, they were planted in a grid like structure, from the coastal ports to the interior areas of where the desired commodities existed. Railways therefore did not link areas away from the ports that could have been more fruitful for the internal development of those colonies.

Later Economic Policies

Africans served extensively in the Second World War, fighting besides their colonial rulers. The war revealed how dependent the European countries were on African supplies. Furthermore, the French African territories had been largely sucked dry by taxation and extraction and it was reported that just before the war there was a need for infusion of capital if any further gains were to be had from the colonies. The war held down action on this report. Thus for all of these circumstances, after the war, both Britain and France decided to inject some capital into their African colonies.

The British government passed two Colonial Development and Welfare Acts (CD &W) in 1940 and 1945 to provide this funding. The French in 1946 instituted the FIDES funds (*Fonds d'investissement pour le développement économique et social*). In the British colonies these were largely matching funds. For example, Sierra Leone was expected to spend 5.2 million pounds sterling on projects and only 2.9 million was to come from the CD &W funds. The French provision was in sum much larger than that of the British.

Most of the monies provided overall went to projects controlled by Europeans like mining concerns or white settler farming in Kenya and Rhodesia. Some of it went to improve production of crops favorable to the colonial rulers like the Djazira irrigation scheme that increased cotton production in the Sudan or the British groundnut scheme in Tanganyika which failed. None of these monies were spent to improve peasant farmer production that could have contributed towards a better food supply in the colonies.

A small portion however did go towards the improving of the physical condition of a few schools with new buildings. A few hospitals were also built in the main administrative headquarters while a smidgen was involved mainly with disease prevention.

Neglected Areas

Apart from peasant farming, one of the most neglected areas in the colonies was industrial development. There was a clear determination that African colonies were to be retained solely as a source for raw materials. Therefore, industry was actively discouraged. A few examples will suffice here.

In British controlled Egypt, the most prominent British administrator there was Lord Cromer who ruled Egypt from 1883 to 1922. Cromer is credited with having brought financial order to Egypt and improved cotton production. Seen from a different perspective, what Cromer did was for the benefit of Britain at the expense of the Egyptians. Since cotton was Egypt's main crop, a group of English entrepreneurs wanted to start manufacturing cloth out of this cotton in Egypt. Cromer killed the industry by levying the same tariff on any goods manufactured locally in Egypt as was levied on imported goods. The progressive procedure would have been to encourage such new industry with lower tariffs. A fledgling cotton industry could therefore not compete with the imported cloth. Cromer also placed high tariffs on imported coal, the fuel needed to support industrial production in Egypt.

Another example involved the manufacture of rope in Tanganyika. The sisal plant, used for this purpose, grew well in Tanganyika. A few of the British plantation owners therefore set up a rope-making factory there in 1937. When the African produced rope reached the British market, rope manufacturers in England cried foul. The British colonial office responded by re-asserting the principle that African colonies must be confined to the production and export of raw materials.

These were not isolated examples. In Sierra Leone, the British waived taxes on imported goods while taxing similar locally produced goods, thus stifling production of the latter. A local entrepreneur in Sierra Leone, Dr. Abayomi Cole, was banned from the local manufacture of tobacco, brandy, soap and sugar in the early twentieth century. The colonial government also gave huge subsidies to a European company to manufacture soft drinks in Sierra Leone. When a local business, the Freetown Mineral Water Company, applied for such assistance from the government, it was denied. Throughout the British colonies, the local distillation of liquor was banned and many people were put in jail for distilling what the colonial ruler labeled as 'injurious spirit.' Yet production of these same local liquor was promoted by the end of the colonial rule, to be refined and sold sometimes by European entrepreneurs

Thus the development of peasant agricultural production or industry either received no support or actually regressed during colonial rule in Africa.

Evaluation of the Benefits of Colonial Rule for Africans

What did Africans gain out of colonial rule? It has often been argued that in spite of all its flaws, Africans were net gainers from the colonial experience. In terms of social infrastructure, the promotion of schools, hospitals and similar benefits, these were meager. The few hospitals built had the best of their facilities reserved for Europeans in the colonies. Education was largely at the primary level but even this was deficient. By 1960, it is estimated that only three or four percent of African teenagers were in high schools. It was worse in some colonies than in others. In the French colony of Guinea for instance, by 1955, three years before independence, there was only one hospital in the capital, Conakry, serving the whole colony. There were two ambulances, twenty dispensaries and fifteen midwife posts. These latter two involved Africans trained to dispense first aid or to attend to the basics of maternity.

One could perhaps mention the hooking up of African colonies to the world economy that was most effectively done in the colonial period. This was however not done for the benefit of the Africans as they had no say in determining how they were aligned with the world economy. African peoples were brought in as appendages, producing and exporting only what raw materials interested the Europeans, while importing cheap manufactured goods from Europe. A situation of grave dependence was therefore being created for African countries by this development.

Ethiopia

In order to properly relate to the question of whether Africans should be grateful for whatever colonial rule brought to them, one needs to consider developments in Ethiopia. Ethiopia spared itself colonization at the end of the nineteenth century by defeating Italy, the European country claiming Ethiopia as her colony, at the Battle of Adowa in 1896. Italy nursed her wounds and returned in 1935 with the compliance of the other European powers and conquered Ethiopia, to rule that nation until the Second World War. During that war, Italy was fighting on the side of Germany against Britain and her allies. British support enabled Ethiopia to free herself again from colonial rule.

Thus for the first third of the twentieth century, Ethiopia was a free and independent country. The rulers of Ethiopia particularly set upon a program to develop their country. This was started under the Emperor Menelik. Concessions for a Railway were granted in 1894, but the line only went twenty-three miles by 1915. A national currency was established in 1894 while telegraph lines were set up as well as banks, hostels and modern roads built. The first cabinet was announced in 1907. Ethiopia had a postal system and joined the International Postal Union in 1908 in spite of stiff opposition by some of the European powers.

These reforms were built on by Ras Tafari during his regency (1917–1928) and when he later assumed the position of emperor with the name Haile Sellasie. Tafari established a Ministry of Commerce and a department of Public Works in 1922. He set up a printing press purchased from Germany in 1923, printing a newspaper; as well as religious and educational books, mostly in Amharic, the main language of Ethiopia.

In order to take advantage of the collective security provided by the League of Nations, formed in 1919 after the First World War, Tafari applied to join the League. He was hotly opposed by most European powers, especially Britain, on the grounds that slavery still continued in Ethiopia. Tafari used every state power to abolish slavery to the satisfaction of the European powers so that, even though Britain still opposed, Ethiopia was admitted to the League in 1923.

Tafari visited Europe in that same year and Ethiopia became alive to the need for utilizing European inventions. Several motorcars were purchased, increasing the fleet of motor vehicles in Addis Ababa, the capital, to several hundreds. Youths were sent for higher education to different countries in Europe. A new hospital was set up in 1924 run by a Swede. Modern schools were established, some run by Europeans, teaching French, English, Amharic and scientific subjects, which displeased traditionalists. Concessions were given to Europeans to build new roads and bridges; aircrafts were bought as Tafari overcame the traditionalist opposition of the nobility.

While developments were delayed by the world depression in the 1920s and 1930s which reduced exports, Haile Sellasie pressed on with his plan. In 1931, the foreign owned bank of Abyssinia was replaced by a national bank, and a written constitution was enacted in that same year. A powerful radio station was set up in 1935, by which time there were fourteen government schools with thirty foreign teachers and about 4,000 students in Addis Ababa alone. As one Italian physician said of Menelik, 'if an adventurer proposed to erect an escalator to the moon the emperor would ask him to build it, if only to see if it could be done.' Christian missionary effort was also evident, running schools and addressing local diseases. A new salaried civil service was established staffed with students returning home from studies in Europe.

Ethiopia then was moving in the direction of modernization, making its own stumbling steps in the process, before the Italian invasion. The details would show that her progress seemed better than those of other African territories under colonial rule at the same time. In fact Ethiopia was taking progressive steps other African countries are only now struggling to implement, like printing literature and pursuing education in the indigenous languages.

It is difficult then to see why colonial rule would be regarded as having been most beneficial to Africa when it forced an extremely disadvantageous path of modernization on its peoples, one that Africa has found it difficult to correct into the twenty first century.

Questions

1. Discuss colonial attitudes and policy towards African agriculture during colonial rule.
2. Can one argue that the benefits of colonial rule to Africa are overstated?

Chapter V

℘ℂℜ

Social Change: Christianity, Western Education and Urbanization

To discuss social change is to talk about issues that are not readily quantifiable. Most significantly, it is an evaluation of changes in attitudes that determine how people choose or regard options about the various values that govern their lives. Changes in attitudes often imply free will decisions about options. Before such free will decisions are arrived at however, there could have been a period of sustained coercion or tremendous pressure that could determine such choice and consequently the direction of change. The latter possibility is the story of social change brought about by colonial rule.

One often implied assumption in the discussions of social change in Africa during the colonial period is the idea of change from a traditionalist, retrogressive to a modern, progressive situation ushered in by the forces of colonial rule. Nothing could be farther away from the truth. African peoples on the main accommodated the new values of colonial rule to their own African systems. Thus what emerged was often a dual perspective, a combining of western and African ways, with however a predominant value being placed on western ways.

The most significant element of social change in the colonial period was the emergence of an urban, westernized middle class. The most prominent badge of this group was its attitude that things western were by far superior to things African. This attitude was a product of the persistent indoctrination of colonial rule. The middle class which emerged from this period represented those who had been most influenced by the two most powerful forces of change in this period, western education and western Christianity, the two being often combined.

The importance of this impact was that the urban bourgeoisie, though not particularly liked by the colonial rulers, became the inheritors of relative prosperity through positions given by the colonial rulers, and most significantly of political power at the end of colonial rule. Throughout the colonial period, Africans were conditioned to believe that western education, Christianity and attendant western values were the key to advancement. When achieved, this was rewarded in the colonial system with what were then regarded as prominent jobs in the service of the colonial rulers. Those Africans who held these jobs then became the pace setters, the reference point for the rest of the population. The actions and affectations of these now powerful Africans became objects of envy and emulation by the rest of the population. The African bourgeoisie was thus put in a position to lead or mislead the rest of the population. To follow then the emergence of this middle class, we need to look more closely at these forces of change.

Western Education

The introduction of western education came largely through missionary effort facilitated by the colonial authorities. Of course, in certain areas like Ethiopia and parts of North Africa, local initiative had taken steps to introduce western education in order to reduce the technological gap existing between theirs and western societies.

On the main however, this work was done by European Christian missionaries, eager to save the souls of Africans, as they saw their task. Missionary work had actually started in some areas, particularly along the coast, before the end of the nineteenth century. Christian missions had however scored little success before the colonial conquest which enhanced their activities. Missionaries, who had been worried about their safety in attempting to penetrate the interior, were now protected by the umbrella of colonial rule and therefore moved in with much greater gusto. When they did not score much initial success with converting adults, they realized that starting with children was a less obtrusive way and one which ascertained that by adulthood, those children would help to propagate the Christian religion.

Missionaries offered western education and technical training as an attraction to convince parents to send their children to school. In some areas, like among the Nguni of South Africa, the school idea was first introduced before the Church element accompanied it. In other instances, particularly in strongly Islamic areas where the population was more adamant about sending their children to Christian schools, colonial governments did set up some schools.

Colonial governments had a vested interest in giving some of their African subjects basic education, so that they could provide manpower to fill particularly clerical positions for which it was uneconomical to import manpower from Europe. Thus even in places where government schools were not opened, the missionary schools were provided with subsidies, protection and land by the colonial authorities to further their work.

There was a sluggish start and lack of strong initial interest on the part of most colonial subjects for this new education. In many areas, youngest sons, those considered pariah or of low social status were the first sent to such schools, as leaders of local communities still regarded the new colonial masters with some defiance and distrust. In time, as the benefits of the education were seen in the response to its products of the colonial rulers, some local African communities began to take a strong interest, some, like the Gikuyu of Kenya, setting up their own schools.

Nature of Education Provided

The education provided was largely primary education. Above that level, the first consideration was higher institutions to train priests and Church auxiliaries. Thus a few mission colleges were set up like Fourah Bay College in Sierra Leone, Livingstonia Mission in Nyasaland and Lovedale in South Africa. One of the first concerns of some of these missionary institutions of higher education was to translate the Bible into the local languages. This was prominent at Lovedale. This was to ensure that the gospel got home to the local people and Christianity would be more readily implanted. In consequence, the Bible became the most widely read literature among Africans in South Africa. But this innovation was not taken beyond this stage of translating the Bible. African countries are still struggling with the introduction of mother tongue education. By the late colonial period, after the Second World War, a few high schools and in British colonies a couple of colleges had been set up.

The curriculum in all schools was entirely western. Imbued with the conviction of racial superiority, the western instructors deliberately taught the African pupils that their values were barbarous and backward. The education did not teach about African values, only seeking at every opportunity to point out that these were not worthy of advancement or progress. On the other hand, everything western was extolled. Africans educated in this system did not know for a long time that many Europeans were also poor, some superstitious, slothful, etc. All Europeans were held to be superior while European societies, which Africans were taught about, were all paved with gold. Education did not teach about two mangoes, found in Africa, and two others making four; with left over books from European schools, it instructed that two peaches, which African children knew nothing about, and two more gave four. The songs taught to the pupils, about "Frère Jacque" and "London bridge is falling down", made no sense to the children, except to create a mystique of some awesome societies from whence their European teachers originated. A few years into the educational system was enough to get African children turning against their own cultures while regarding the white teachers and the countries they came from as the most desirable people and places in the world. These were the future leaders of Africa.

Christianity and African Religion

We already mentioned that Christian missionary activity was given a greater impetus by the colonial conquest and establishment of colonial rule. The mutuality of interest between the colonial government and the missionaries did not end there, for each aided the other in spreading the message of domination and control.

Christian missions sprang up in all parts of Africa beyond the coast as colonial rule effectively advanced. First staffed by European missionaries, these missions were increasingly supported or run by African auxiliaries, especially after the first couple of decades of colonial rule. As European missionaries went to live in the interior, they became more and more knowledgeable about African customs and used this knowledge to further the entrenchment of Christianity. What we need to appreciate most poignantly is that Christian missions were not solely carrying the message of religion. Christianity to these missionaries was synonymous with western culture. Thus they sought to convert Africans to both. This process of conversion meant separating Africans from the strong link between their own culture and religion, as missionaries taught Africans that life could be separated into the religious and secular spheres, a concept alien to virtually all African cultures.

For the determination of the missionaries to spread western culture and Christianity to work, they had to have an equal urge to stamp out adherence to African culture in their converts. African life and ritual were intricately bound. Most African societies believed in one supreme God, rendered by different names. This God was worshipped through spirit mediums, priests and priestesses, and ritual, considered important on every occasion, dominated African life. Thus to tell Africans to separate religion from everyday life was an extremely tall order.

Yet this is what the missionaries sought to achieve and substitute Christianity and western ways for African religions. The missionaries preached that only the God in the Bible was the true God and all the African Gods were false. The Church, they insisted, was the only source of divine grace and salvation of mankind. All African religions were therefore explicitly condemned by these missionaries as 'pagan.' The Bible was interpreted by the missionaries to give Africans the impression that Europeans were the chosen race and Africans were the condemned. It was these condemned Africans that the Europeans had come to save. The Church thus consistently supported colonial policies meant to 'save' Africans, to turn them away from their cultural practices and get them to follow European ways that would benefit the determination for exploitation. The Dutch Calvinist Church in South Africa, for example, was one of the staunchest supporters and promoters of apartheid and its hatred and degradation of Africans.

The work of the missionaries did not stop at the assault on African religion. To fulfill their mission, all of African culture had to be condemned. Traditional practices like drumming and dancing, rite of passage ceremonies, customs related to birth and death, pouring of libation and a host of other cultural values were condemned as barbaric, including African names. Thus to be a Christian, Africans had to give up all of these 'barbaric' practices, adopt western culture and a new western name and turn their backs on their own culture. This is what missionary work in Africa was about.

It was not easy for missionaries to achieve this kind of transformation as Africans resisted. In Senegal, for example, Muslims had rebelled to retain their legal system in the framework of early French assimilation policy. Many who became Christians were ostracized particularly at the initial phases, and everything possible was done to preserve traditional life and religion. But the missionaries were relentless, and they had the full support of the colonial government which enforced laws to ban certain African custom which they could not get rid of by other methods. The colonial government and the missionaries were on the same page. They were both trying to control Africans and get them to support western rule and system in every way. Thus they worked together.

This collusion was evident everywhere. One of the most abhorrent elements of African culture to the missionaries was female initiation ceremonies which involved clitoridectomy. The issue came out more forcefully in East Africa. The missions had some difficulty relating to the incision on the penis done in the male initiation ceremonies. They adjusted to this however, only insisting that it be done in hospitals or private homes. Perhaps the adjustment here had to do with the persistence of similar circumcision in western society, derived from Jewish culture. Female circumcision had to be stamped out as unchristian.

The matter surfaced more prominently in the 1920s among the Gikuyu of Kenya, already swamped by many missionary units and the loss of their land. While the mission schools taught anti-African values, the Gikuyu set up their own schools to take in children rejected from Christian schools because of female circumcision. In 1929, the Gikuyu developed a dance song called ***muthirigu*** to ridicule Christian converts and their opposition to female circumcision. The song became so popular that the colonial government issued a law banning the song in 1930. When the Gikuyu set up their own independent Church, the African Orthodox Church, preaching impending doom for Europeans and their missions, the colonial government also banned the Church.

Similar action by colonial authorities elsewhere made missionary work more successful. In the Gold Coast, the colonial government moved to suppress some religious rituals and deities. In 1907, the deity of the Akim Kotoku people, for example, was prohibited from operating by law. The German colonial government destroyed the shrines of the cult of Dente in Kete Krachi in Togo colony in the 1880s. In Uganda in 1912, laws were passed by the British colonial government banning traditional practices associated with 'witchcraft' in an obvious effort to proscribe traditional religions practices. The laws were beefed up in 1921 with stiffer penalties.

Apart from the support of the colonial government, missionaries also used their advanced medical skills to convince Africans that salvation only lay with the Christian doctrine. The missionary organizations also set up hospitals where it was impressed upon Africans that Christianity was blended with the healing process.

As indicated earlier, this Christian indoctrination was blended with western education so that its most forceful impact was on the impressionable minds of the young. As colonial rule advanced however, the attraction of the medical, educational and other technical skills taught by the missionaries began to show fruit in greater, relatively improved material prosperity of the new converts. Christianity thus came to have more adherents and new converts became an important vehicle in the extension of Christianity further a-field in the colonies.

Urbanization

The erosion of African culture under the impact of colonial rule was much more obvious in the towns that grew up in the colonial system. While Africa had urban centers before colonial rule, their numbers increased dramatically in the colonial period. By 1931, for example, the population of Dakar had grown dramatically to 54,000, Accra to 60,000, Addis Ababa to 65,000, Nairobi to 48,000, to name a few.

Several factors supported this new urbanization process. One of the main elements was the location of the seat of the colonial rulers. These colonial capitals grew very quickly as the attraction of the source of power and opportunities lured migrants. The European official (and settler) population was concentrated in these capitals and therefore, jobs supporting the colonial administration were more prevalent there. The slim infrastructural elements like hospitals, occasional high schools, main offices of trading houses, were concentrated at these capitals. It is for these reasons that post colonial capitals generally bore the stamp of a central place, for they were usually much larger and more important than any second tier towns. Thus the attraction of jobs and higher education were largely to be found at the capital. Second tier towns also grew up around mining areas or provincial headquarters, at major railway stations or road heads.

Apart from the possibilities for employment, these towns carried other attractions. The bright lights of the cities, cinema halls and other urban fascinations brought by colonial rule tended to lure fortune and thrill seekers to the towns. As migrants established residences in the big towns, they tended to attract 'brothers and sisters,' members of the extended family or clan from the rural areas to their residences in the towns. Thus one came to have concentrations of specific ethnic populations growing up around and thereby enlarging the towns.

The big towns were the areas where colonial governments were most able to enforce their values and domination. New laws and pronouncements could be more easily disseminated in the towns and enforced there where a police force and colonial might was more visible. This atmosphere, combined with Christianity and other elements of western culture, produced a new situation in the towns. The concentration of different ethnic and cultural elements with a dominant overlay of western culture came to dominate the cities. It is here that the westernized African middle class grew more readily and was more comfortable. This was the place where they were likely to find most of the trappings of western culture they held so dear. Unlettered migrants looked on the elite as role models, but had to stick to their own cultural values that were somewhat modified by the prevalent western influence. Thus one finds ethnic organizations and Churches growing at the capitals, blending western and traditional modes of dispensing justice, support and religion. Specifically ethnic courts were set up, sometimes opposed by the colonial administration. Community organization provided support for clan events including rites of passage ceremonies surrounding birth, marriage and death.

Urbanization and Matrilineal Societies

Another factor that stimulated urbanization, particularly in southern Africa was the imposition of a European patriarchal system on predominantly matrilineal societies. Most of the dominant Bantu ethnic groups in Central and Southern Africa like the Chewa of Malawi, the Gikuyu of Kenya, the Bemba of Zambia and the peoples of the Kongo kingdom were matrilineal systems, reckoning succession to positions of power, ownership of land, inheritance to property, through the mother. Many of the local rulers and officials in this region, sometimes referred to as the matrilineal belt, were female.

With the advent of colonial rule, the Europeans approached these female rulers in search of labor to build particularly roads and railways. Europeans refused to accept female labor when offered and selected the men who were then moved from their homes to new work sites. This was the beginning of migrant labor which became so significant in the mines of South Africa.

These male workers now found new locations in these new work sites that often grew up into big towns. In these new centers, the men could now own land and build their own houses, while in the traditional setting the land was held by the women. These new male, urban landowners therefore became wedded to the colonial system that provided them with new power and property, a new place in the new urban centers they could now regard as belonging to them.

Migration to urban centers for men, later for western education and consequently the powerful jobs in the colonial system, then came to represent a disruption and distortion of the existing structure of matrilineal societies that were now replaced by the colonial patriarchal system. This new system gradually wound up in the new 'tradition', having been legitimized by colonial rule.

Cultural Transformations

The lure of the cities was not always favorable to migrants. Many went to the urban areas in search of jobs or excitement. While still attached to traditional culture and religion at the outset, a migrant might not readily find a place to practice these elements, while she was pressured by the attractions of the new urban culture. Gradually, she might 'wander' into a Church organization or some urban social club where she learns new values, more relevant to her new place of residence. In such ways, migrants were acculturated into the emergent urban culture with its western cultural overlay.

All of these factors acted on each other to produce a situation where by the late colonial period, western culture, Christianity and western education were becoming accepted as the means of advancement and progress, and this thinking was by then warmly embraced by the new middle class. This was precisely the goal of the colonial rulers which they struggled to force down the throats of initially unwilling colonial subjects at the start of colonial rule. They had largely succeeded by the Second World War.

We should remember that this process did not begin operating at the beginning of the twentieth century in all parts of Africa. Colonial rule had started often a couple of decades earlier in some areas. Algeria had been colonized since 1830 by the French. A small enclave of what is today Sierra Leone had become a British colony almost a century before 1900. A Krio middle class had emerged there by that time, and this group was active in spreading colonialist values throughout the other British colonies in west Africa like Nigeria and the Gold Coast, as they had a head start in getting jobs in the colonial service in those colonies. A British Gold Coast colony had been established since the 1870s, around the same time that the Congo Free State was set up by Leopold of Belgium. Of course South Africa also was a British colony throughout the nineteenth century and the presence of a strong white settler population was pervasive in entrenching these values.

This development had therefore started well before the twentieth century and the onset of colonial rule in most areas at the end of the nineteenth century reinforced and rapidly expanded this system and philosophy.

The Contemporary African City

An urban African culture consequently developed particularly in the capital cities of African countries. It is marked by a blend of African and western values. The emphasis on western attributes is evident since this is regarded as the yardstick of being considered progressive. African cultural elements are increasingly acquiring a strong expression in this mix as many urban Africans later came to grips with their cultural heritage.

This blend is seen in dress forms where African flavored cotton prints are used to fashion African style dresses that are worn with western style shoes and adornments. Western type fabric is also used to make outfits of the Mao Tse Tung style or what western society regards as leisure suits for men. All of these fashions are increasingly being adopted by the elite even though in the end they come out more expensive to acquire. The rest of the urban population also adopt a blend of these styles and cheaper western style dress as they can afford. A distinctly Islamic style of dress alongside those described here, with Islamic robes is also discernible in many African cities

In music, bands with mostly western musical instruments like the guitar develop songs with basic African rhythms blended with western derived harmonic and melodic inventions. These are mostly sung in African languages or a combination of these languages and those of the former colonial rulers. Most frequently they use African languages and throw in phrases in English or French, virtually replicating the way urban Africans relate to these languages. Thus 'African' songs in English, French or Portuguese are common in most urban African music. A recurrent theme in many urban African songs is a critique of life in the city for the rural newcomer. The most popular of these songs across sub-Saharan Africa are those sung in the Lingala language from the Democratic Republic of the Congo and Juju music sung in Yoruba and pidgin English from Nigeria.

Though the former colonial languages remain those employed for official issues, particularly in the urban areas, various adaptations of these languages have developed. These develop syntax and incorporate vocabulary from African languages in varying degrees. Thus it is possible to talk about West African English or French, for example. Over time, some of these adaptations or 'pidgins' develop into languages in their own right. To hear Nigerian pidgin English being spoken would leave a native English speaker mesmerized.

Urban African culture also carries a strong underlay of African religious values even though Christianity and then Islam are the dominant ones. Even though indigenous African religions are considered 'backward' by the western trained, many of these same elite elements who regard themselves as Christian or Muslim still visit African religious diviners for charms and amulets and concoctions believed to empower them to win elections or for women to win or keep wealthy consorts. The big difference in this practice is that the urban elite will do this in secret, ready to vehemently deny that they believe in these African religious values. This evidently is an expression of entrenched cultural values publicly frowned upon by the same bourgeoisie whose western orientation is what they think must be emphasized

Questions

1. What role did Christianity play in the emergence of an African middle class?
2. Identify and comment on the elements of an African urban culture.

Chapter VI

ഗ്ര

The Psychological Impact of Colonialism

What has been examined in the previous chapter represents the main vehicles of indoctrination of Africans in the colonial period—western education and Christianity, and how these played predominantly in the main urban areas. But these factors alone are inadequate in explaining the change of attitude experienced by African peoples, eventually turned away from their own cultures to become unquestioning followers of western values. The situation accomplished by colonial rule, of alienating Africans from their own culture, was fostered and reinforced by a number of other factors. These included an assault on a variety of cultural elements like dress, food, language use, music, issues we want to consider here.

The assault on these elements was made using a variety of approaches including the force of law and regulation, ridicule applied by a new colonial master on conquered subjects, the misapplication of western technology to imply superiority of other aspects of western culture, and other similar methods. In the end, led by the African bourgeoisie, Africans became convinced that all aspects of their cultures were debased and every element of western culture was superior. While most Africans still practiced elements of their traditional values, they took every opportunity to demonstrate a longing to be regarded as accomplished, to be westernised. The African elite became of course almost totally lost to African culture, regarding it on the main as amusement, just like the Europeans did. The elite still however ate some African foods and followed a few African values intermittently. Let us examine the process of distortion of African values which led to this state of alienation.

Colonial Conquest

One issue not often closely examined is the impact of the military conquest which ushered in colonial rule. Psychologically, people in any society would come to develop respect if not admiration for another group which defeats yours mercilessly, sometimes repeatedly, as happened to Africans when they regrouped and rebelled against colonial rule. In this case, those who defeated Africans did not leave; they stayed on as the new rulers. The psychology of defeat resulting from the conquest paved the way significantly for the implantation of other values by the colonial conquerors.

The colonial military conquest in itself was also very disastrous to other elements basic to African cultures. The conquest destroyed the power of the indigenous political and military rulers, the leaders of society. There was no way that African power and prestige could be reinstated under the new dispensation of colonial rule. The former African elite therefore suffered the shaken faith of their peoples in their mighty power, the loss of their positions and professions as rulers and military leaders, and the attendant loss of income and status. This was particularly marked in areas where these old leaders were removed or severely restricted in the new offices they acquired from the colonial conquerors.

The military resistance had also been actively supported, often led by those who controlled traditional religion and ritual. We have noted earlier how they boosted morale among the resistors by strengthening them with the belief that they would be invincible to European bullets. The disastrous defeat of the armies so emboldened, the realization that the ritual protection was ineffective, could only have shaken the foundations of traditional religion. These religious leaders also lost their dominant positions as they were not recognized, in fact often punished by the new colonial rulers. Even though religion has a way of satisfactorily explaining away its own failures, the weakened faith in the powers of their priests, some of whom were captured and publicly executed, could only have been a forceful blow to traditional religion. And this occurred precisely at the time when Christian missionaries were poised to pounce on these societies to reinforce these doubts.

Thus, as the erstwhile leaders of societies in Africa adjusted to new roles, drastically reduced incomes, bewildered Africans could only have been less tenacious in their resistance to the new religion and culture of their new rulers, where theirs had failed.

African Names and Dress

The colonial impact affected most areas of society. An important issue was that of dress. Particularly in sub-Saharan Africa, the tropical climate and agricultural pursuits encouraged a culture of being scantily dressed. This pattern of dress was described by the new colonial rulers as barbaric. In a variety of ways and not merely by example, Africans were encouraged to wear western style clothing instead of their own dress fashions. An incident occurred in the Sierra Leone colony in 1806 where a Muslim trader and broker named Dala Modu, whom the colonial government had been used to trading with, was charged with slave trading. In appearance before the British governor of the colony, he put on an Islamic robe he was used to wearing in his more local activities. This was seen as an act of defiance by the governor and Modu was expelled from the colony. His attire had to be western before he could properly address the British governor.

In virtually all colonies, particularly British, the colonial rulers developed the practice of regarding African dress, no matter now attractive, as 'costume.' This of course meant that on festive occasions or to do a play in school, it was acceptable for people to wear these costumes, meaning their traditional dress. Africans later began to refer to their indigenous dress styles as costumes with the implication that these could not be worn on 'official and respectable occasions.' Of course, in none of the schools set up by missionaries or government were children allowed to wear any kind of indigenous dress styles. Europeans and the new elite after them took every opportunity to deride African dress and promote proper, meaning western dress. Gradually everyone in the colonies came to believe that to be properly dressed was to wear western attire while one could amuse oneself with costumes or African dress.

A similar situation occurred in many colonies in regard to African names which especially missionaries discouraged in their converts. African names were not Christian—only western names were. So, once baptized, a convert had to assume a 'Christian' name. The term 'first name' was not used, at least in British African colonies. One had a 'Christian' and a 'surname.' Several writings by Europeans in the colonial period referred to African names as 'barbaric.'

Due to this attitude of the colonialists to African names, a spate of name changing occurred in many African societies under colonial rule. In the Islamic community in Freetown, the capital of Sierra Leone, urban Muslims began to assume western last names added to their Islamic first names. In applying for jobs, they tried to disguise their first names, often by using initials. Other peoples accommodated by giving two names to their children. The first name was the 'official' or 'Christian' name, and a second African name, used in non-formal or domestic situations. Western trained Africans in particular would not use the African second names even where they had been given at birth. They had come to believe, as taught by their European teachers, that these names were retrogressive.

Language Use and Education

One important area in which African values were assailed was in that of languages. Usually, to the untrained ear, a totally new language sounds rather strange. Add to this racial prejudice and it will become clear why Europeans came to regard African languages as uncivilized. Africans were discouraged from using their indigenous languages outside their localized activities; this latter domain the colonial ruler had no power over. Everywhere else Africans came to realize that they had to use the language of the colonial rulers or they would have no benefits in the colonial system.

As mentioned before, Africans used to be mostly independent farmers. The colonial system ensured that many of them had to find jobs and the colonial rulers or their surrogates—European plantation owners or mining concerns, controlled virtually all the available jobs. An individual's chances of getting a job were greatly enhanced if he could understand the European language or, better still speak even a smattering of it. This desire to acquire the language of the new rulers as a ticket to advancement became an important reason for migration to urban centers. There one had at least a brushing with the European language of the rulers and learnt probably a pidginized form of it, getting thus nearer to employment.

This ban on the use of African languages, whether official or unofficial, was nowhere more obvious than in the school systems. Punishment was meted out to pupils who spoke their indigenous languages in school, whether it was Gikuyu in Kenya, Temne in Sierra Leone or Wolof in Senegal. The language of instruction was entirely that of the colonial rulers and pupils had to struggle through learning both the new language and the concepts that came with the new education. In most African countries, until independence and beyond, virtually all education was in the European languages. The teachers, both European and African, could not be seen in indigenous dress nor speaking local languages.

Those educated in this system soon came away with the mistaken notion that it was impossible to be educated if one did not speak a European language. In addition, it became a common idea that it was demeaning to speak African languages in formal or important social occasions. Worse still, it came to be thought that education in these European languages was only about things that happened in the European countries from whence these languages came. The implication drawn from this was that things African were not the subject of education. This thinking was reinforced by the fact that there was nothing about Africa being taught in the curriculum in the schools. Nowhere was African history taught. In fact students were taught to believe that Africans had no history and this dictum was repeated by learned professors in the European countries where a few Africans went to study right down into independence in Africa in the 1960s. Africans could only learn about the 'pacification' of Africa by Europeans to end 'tribal' wars and slavery. All of these factors only served to get Africans to lose confidence in their culture, the very foundations of their being.

A few missionaries and colonial officials did learn African languages and cultures in the relatively isolated mission stations where they were located. The missionaries used this knowledge to further the advancement of their Christian conversion, translating the Bible into African languages so that Africans could better be indoctrinated. Missionaries did not teach in or about African languages in the schools they set up.

Clearly, these products of the colonial system who became the rulers in Africa at independence never even dreamt that it was necessary or useful to do anything with African languages as far as education and advancement were concerned. To even speak their African languages began to appear as a burden to them after they had become acculturated into western values.

Other Areas of Contact

The same deliberate distortions associated with western education, language, dress were also true of the assault on other aspects of African culture. African music was considered lousy, too loud, as if that was offensive and unacceptable. African dance was lewd and indecent. Having developed in a tropical environment, African life was especially an outdoor life. Music tended therefore to be louder than western music for example, as it was almost always played outdoors. To the colonizers, however, it was uncivilized because it was loud. African foods and dishes were regarded as being unfit for classy occasions. This factor became so embedded in the minds of urban Africans that they often resorted to western dishes for special occasions. Thus one still finds far more western dishes than African ones in many hotels and restaurants in African cities.

The demeaning policies of colonial rule were also evident in the area of employment. Africans had to be given only low paying jobs; if they received wages similar to whites, it would be inconsistent with the aura of superiority of the colonial rulers and inferiority of the Africans that colonial rule taught. While most Africans received very low pay and menial jobs in the colonial system, a very few slipped through the cracks, went to the colonial capitals and acquired a high degree of western education and professional training and qualified as doctors, lawyers and accountants. As the colonial service was the greatest employer in formal sector employment, most of these had to take jobs in the colonial service. Since lawyers soon went into private practice, the discrimination in highly placed positions became most evident in the employment and conditions of service of African doctors in the colonial system. Apart from being paid less than their white counterparts, medical doctors in the British colonial service in Africa were relegated to relatively lower positions above which they could not advance. No African doctor had a rank higher than any white doctor in the service. The colonial authorities went so far as to circulate false information that British people did not want to be treated by African doctors.

Resultant Impact

There were two major results of this combined attack on the African colonial subjects. The first was that the entire process ended with Africans coming to feel themselves inferior to Europeans, no matter how well educated or accomplished the Africans were. Thus accomplishment was defined only in western terms and with western values for, as indicated earlier, all things African were considered backward.

For the African to consider herself accomplished therefore, she had to distance herself as far as possible from her African milieu. This was the underlying statement of French and Portuguese assimilation. Thus the more prosperous the western educated Africans became in the eyes of their less favored brothers and sisters, the more the elite felt good about distancing themselves from their culture and societies.

The second problem was that the successful African now became, within a couple of decades of colonial rule, the role model to other Africans living in the rural areas. Africans in these rural regions sought that at least their children should become like these 'enlightened' brethren who had important jobs in the cities or were successful there. This successful urban African now became a leader in condemning African culture as inferior to his rural kinsmen since his success was predicated on his association with western culture and his distance from African values. By the late colonial period, it was no longer necessary for the colonial authorities to continue emphasizing to Africans how backward African culture was, though they did not stop doing so. The African bourgeoisie now did a better job of that vilification.

As the colonial period drew to a close by the 1950s, it became evident to these westernized African middle class that they would likely become the inheritors of political power from the colonial rulers. In their understanding, the African middle class had acquired this ability to inherit political power through their successful movement through the processes necessary to fulfill the colonial perception of advancement. They were now poised to control the unaccomplished masses. The African bourgeoisie now sought to take every opportunity to mystify the average African about this wonderful knowledge of the western world that had ensured them their position of prominence. What they did not understand about the western world they explained away, sometimes in the most mysterious ways, only serving to righteously mesmerize the masses.

A majority of the elite had only acquired a very limited level of western education and exposure. Many of those in the first parliaments in independent Africa were those trained in the mission stations as catechists and primary school teachers. They had usually acquired western education no further than middle high school levels. But they were adored by their brethren from the rural environment, particularly with their newly found political power.

This attitude of the bourgeoisie of knowing it all and therefore being qualified to speak for the masses was to be extremely harmful to African progress after independence, since these ill informed bourgeois rulers of Africa were to often sign away Africa's wealth and independence in contracts they hardly understood. The alienation resulting from the colonial enterprise and their overconfidence about their familiarity with western systems made it easy for western interests to manipulate them with considerable ease.

It is extremely important to highlight this role that colonial rule played in the distorted situation found in Africa today. Most writings had harped on administration, the economy and politics, leaving the reader to believe that these were more important areas in understanding the post colonial situation in Africa. Scholars like Ngugi Wa Thiongo in his *Decolonizing the Mind* and more importantly Frantz Fanon, have tried to draw attention to this most important but neglected area. Fanon, a black West Indian doctor, wrote in French especially two influential works—*Wretched of the Earth* and *Black Skin, White Masks,* before his untimely death at the age of thirty-six. With the Algerian revolution and the colonial impact in the Carribean at the back of his mind, Fanon wrote about the psychological impact of colonialism on colonized peoples, an analysis so incisively analytical of the rest of the African condition. His works have formed a departure point for recent post-colonial critical studies which have sought to examine the impact of imperialism and racism on the cultures and identities of post colonial nations and peoples everywhere. We will return to some of the manifestations of this impact when we come to discuss the post-colonial era.

Questions

1. Present an analysis of the significance of conquest on the ability of colonial rulers to control African peoples during colonial rule.
2. Explain the nature of the contact between African and European languages during colonial rule.

Chapter VII

ಶಂೂ

Protest Movements in the Colonial Era

A s the Twentieth century advanced, Africans accommodated to colonial rule in a variety of ways. Adaptation to political control by new alien rulers was more difficult for some than for others. By the 1920s however, Africans had become used to the idea of colonial rule. Adaptations to the cultural impact of this domination was more optional, but since advancement was now determined largely by an adoption of the values of the colonial ruler, people began assuming these traits, a few embracing them more warmly than others.

As Africans came to learn more about the colonial system, many began to feel the impact of discrimination in wages, promotion on their jobs, more generally in not being treated with respect by the colonial rulers. The African bourgeoisie felt these same setbacks from the colonial authorities, but they too assumed the attitudes of the latter when the opportunity presented itself, and regarded the rest of the population with equal disregard.

Reactions to these problems meant protest of one sort or another. Massive violent protest erupted in some instances, usually ruthlessly put down by the colonial rulers who feared threats to their control. There were also protests that were not violent, amounting to a rejection of the pattern of domination meted out by the colonialists. We want to here examine some of these protest movements throughout colonial rule.

Religion and Protest

One of the areas that was to lend a lot of color to protest was Christianity. Though Christianity reached most Africans with a strong western cultural baggage, it had as its center piece ritual and submission to the will of God. Many Africans, steeped in religion and ritual, transferred this attitude to Christianity and they came to realize its potential in the new dispensation of colonial rule. It became clear to many however that Christianity also came with racial prejudice and discrimination, both in the Church and in relations between the Christian rulers and the subjects newly converted to this religion. Reaction to this treatment varied. For some it was protest in the form of a rejection of the pattern of Christianity brought by the colonial rulers. For others, it was an attempt to use Christianity in ways similar to those adopted by the colonial rulers—to get their own message across to the populace. Those who used Christianity in this latter manner interpreted it in a way that could whip up latent hostility to colonial rule. The colonial rulers caught on to this and stopped it.

Discrimination in the Church was rampant. It included a virtual refusal to recognize the potential of African ministers for leadership of their own people. They should therefore be relegated to junior Church offices. In Nyasaland, for example, Mwase, a candidate for the ministry among the Tonga people, had by 1902 gone through all the necessary rigors to be ordained as a priest. The white run Church refused to ordain him for another ten years.

Such discrimination gradually caused disillusionment and led to priests attempting to set up their own Churches based often on the pattern they had learnt in their Christian training with the white missionaries. This development was very noticeable in southern Africa and was initially influenced by missions set up in the nineteenth century. The Lovedale College in South Africa had trained Sotho Christians who by the 1870s assisted Scottish missionaries in setting up the Livingstonia Mission in Nyasaland. This remained the single most important institution of higher learning in southern Africa well into the twentieth century. It was dedicated to training religious auxiliaries but the process of Christian training also meant acquiring basic education which fit its products for other kinds of service. Graduates of the Livingstonia Mission also traveled southwards into South Africa to work in the mines. They began using their education to lead protest movements.

Nyasaland was also important in spreading elements of religious protest as a result of the influence of an Englishman, Joseph Booth. He encouraged the setting up of independent African churches, particularly of the Watchtower movement. Many of the African church leaders emerging from under his influence spread their activities throughout the entire southern Africa region. John Chilembwe, from Nyasaland, who had accompanied Booth to the United States, set up his own Providence Industrial Mission in 1906. Chilembwe's church attracted a strong following to whom he preached against racial discrimination, culminating in his opposition to the involvement of blacks in the First World War. He led a rising in 1915 in which two whites were killed but the British put down his rebellion and Chilembwe was himself killed in the process.

By far the most widespread movement in this region in this period was the African Watchtower Church founded by Eliot Kamwana by 1909. Deriving inspiration from the American Watchtower movement, Kamwana set up his own system with a strong African consciousness bias. His preaching was appealing to Africans since he advocated millenarian views about the end of the world when white rule would come to an end and blacks would come into their own. The movement did not lead to violent protest, but spread to the neighboring Rhodesias. The British were so alarmed by its wide appeal that they exiled Kamwana from Nyasaland in 1909. He was only allowed to return in 1937.

There were several other independent churches set up by Africans in this region, like the African Methodist Episcopal (AME) Church in Zambia which drew its inspiration from that Church in the United States. Some of these movements used the Church to protest specific aspects of colonial rule. One such was the *Église de Jesus Christ Sur La Terre* founded by the prophet Simon Kimbangu in the Belgian Congo in 1921. Kimbangu encouraged his followers to refuse paying taxes. As the colonial administration intensified forced labor, Kimbangu's followers announced their interest to resists this demand. This threatened the very fabric of Belgian rule in the Congo. Kimbangu was arrested and died in prison in 1951. His followers however continued to expand this mission even into the French Congo and Oubangui-Shari (present Central African Republic). A similar African Orthodox Church in Uganda was founded by an ex-serviceman of the colonial army in Uganda, Reuben Mukasa. Mukasa declared, in opposition to colonial domination, that his church was 'for all right-thinking Africans, men who wish to be free in their own home, not always being thought of as boys.' This church spread to neighboring Kenya.

Independent African Churches also became widespread in other parts of Africa, alarming colonial rulers. A Liberian prophet, William Wade Harris, traveled as an itinerant preacher through the Gold Coast and parts of Côte d'Ivoire between 1910 and 1915. He attracted a large congregation of converts, estimated at some one hundred thousand. The French expelled him from Côte d'Ivoire and he finally remained in the Gold Coast. His preaching and influence led to the formation of the Église Harriste in the Ivory Coast and the Twelve Apostles Church in the Gold Coast.

The nature of protest in some independent Churches amounted to a rejection of many aspects of western culture associated with Christianity, and an indigenization of Christianity. Some of the new Churches set up began to emphasize elements derived from traditional African religions like spirit possession, 'witch finding' and the use of ritually treated water or holy water. This pattern of cultural blend in the African Churches is often described as Zionism. One prominent example of this was the Aladura Church founded in Nigeria by Oshitelu in 1929, which spread to other British African colonies in West Africa. Spirit possession, healing and prophecy, elements strong in African religion, were also very strong in the Zionist Churches in other parts of Africa. *Alfayo Odongo's Joroko* (Holy Ghost) Church founded among the Luo people of Kenya in 1932 also emphasized possession by the spirit and speaking in strange tongues.

Attempts to develop this indigenous Christianity were ridiculed by the African bourgeoisie. In some instances this is what actually led to the formation of separatist Churches. Such was the case with the *Musama Disco Christo* (Army of the Cross of Christ) founded in the Gold Coast by 1922. It had started off as a prayer group within the mainstream Methodist Church in the central region of the Gold Coast. Its Africanized focus was not to the liking of the Methodist Church authorities who expelled the prayer group from the Methodist church in 1919. The prayer group leader, William Egyanhal Appiah then transformed the group into a Church. He organized his Church structure based on the hierarchical principles of the ethnic Akan society of the Gold Coast, setting up as well shrines for healing the sick. This *Musama* Church recognized the existence of demons, witches and evil spirits and sought to demonstrate the power of God over all of these.

These Churches therefore rejected the assumptions of the European missionaries about the link between Christianity and western culture. They sought to demonstrate that Christianity could be immersed in and related to African culture, and thus better serve the needs of the African masses. And indeed independent Churches tended to attract more of the masses just as the Africanity of these Churches tended to turn off the bourgeoisie.

Islam also provided a means of protest under colonial rule. *Mahdism,* the Islamic version of the Christian messiah, became a scourge on the colonial authorities in a number of areas. In all of these communities, the *mahdi* became a symbol of hope and nationalism to the masses. From the Sanusiya Brotherhood in Libya to the Mouriddiyya in Senegal, the colonial authorities always moved against these religious orders and arrested their leaders. Ahmad Bamba, the founder of the indigenous Islamic brotherhood of the Mouridiyya in Senegal, was actually sent into exile by the French for a number of years. In the colony of the Sudan, the British tried to play off the Khatmiyya brotherhood against the Mahdist Ansar movement in an effort to contain both movements. The head of the Khatmiyya brotherhood, Sayyid Ali al-Mirghani, was even knighted by the King of England in 1916, showing British support for this organization as against the Mahdist Ansar.

Trade Unions

Another vehicle of protest in the colonial period was trade unions. This method of collective bargaining by workers was not encouraged in the African colonies. Africans however formed trade unions, often hotly contested by the colonial governments that would at best not recognize such unions, at worst move to stamp them out. It was a bigger problem in the white settler colonies; for while trade unions were recognized among the white settlers, it proved more difficult to forbid trade unions among the black subjects who were emboldened by the white settler unions to start their own.

Trade union activity at its best implied protest. The conditions under which African workers operated during colonial rule only exacerbated the situation. Trade unions therefore became a vehicle for the expression of discontent, focusing on specific labor issues that often spilled over to encompass general dissatisfaction among the populace.

In a number of instances trade unions championed other forms of protest. In South Africa, the Industrial and Commercial Workers Union (ICU) was founded by Klemens Kadalie in 1917 to galvanize the cause of the increasing number of mine workers in the gold mines of South Africa. The ICU did not simply lead strike action on behalf of workers. It led political boycotts as well. In 1929, for example, the ICU branch in Natal was involved in a beer hall boycott which led a white mob to attempt to storm ICU offices. This provoked a series of riots in which six Africans and two whites were killed. In the 1920s, the ICU attempted to set up a branch in Southern Rhodesia. Robert Sambo, who was sent there from South Africa to carry this out was quickly arrested and deported by the colonial government.

In the Copperbelt of Northern Rhodesia (Zambia), African workers were organized enough to stage a series of strike actions against poor conditions and wages. Some of these strikes were accompanied by violent riots and loss of life before colonial troops put them down. In 1940, after white miners got improvement following a strike action, African workers too staged a strike. Violence again erupted and some people lost their lives. In the colony of Sierra Leone, railway workers held strikes in 1919 and 1926 in the face of colonial government opposition to such industrial action. The 1919 strike had degenerated into mass rioting so that in 1926, authorities warned the strikers of dismissal from their jobs. The strike still went on and was supported by the community in Freetown, the capital, which collected funds to support the over two hundred dismissed railway workers.

Trade unions and strikes represented a rallying point for opposition to colonial rule. Their closeness to the masses increased their potential for mob action, while their sense of organization and propriety invited the support of the African bourgeoisie. For precisely these reasons, the colonial governments were always ready to disperse these unions.

Protest and the African Bourgeoisie

Members of the African elite also formed organizations at different levels to protest specific aspects of colonial rule more related to their own hopes and aspirations. Some of these groupings were set up by highly educated Africans with membership largely involving people of their own kind. Many others involved Africans who had had basic education and were either employed in the lower rungs of the colonial service, in mining or by private trading houses in the colonies. While these latter received low incomes compared to the Europeans, they were regarded as members of the elite, particularly in the eyes of their rural folks and urban proletariat. Western education, combined with a basic income, put them in this category and they aspired to improve their status and working conditions with the support of the colonial government. Protest organized by these elite organizations did not often incur the hostility of the colonial governments, as they involved mostly procedures encouraged by the colonialists like petitions, delegations to the authorities, newspaper articles and the like.

One of the most elitist of this type of movement was the National Congress of British West Africa (NCBWA). As its name implies, the NCBWA embraced the leading lights in the British West African colonies of the Gambia, Gold Coast, Nigeria and Sierra Leone. The group which met in 1919 in Accra, the Gold Coast capital, to form this organization was led by J.E. Casely Hayford, a Gold Coast lawyer, and included others like Herbert Macauley from Nigeria and Dr. Bankole Bright from Sierra Leone. Their major demands included no taxation without representation, opposition to discrimination in the colonial service and a certain degree of independently organized institutions like a West African university and press union. Though the colonial government would not listen to them, claiming they were unrepresentative of the masses, the NCBWA continued its existence, meeting at the different West African capitals well into the era of the Second World War.

Apart from this more regional grouping, there were other similar bourgeois organizations in individual colonies like the Aborigines Rights Protection Society in the Gold Coast. On this occasion, the elite and the traditional chief were able to cooperate in opposing a distasteful land law. On rare occasions before the period of decolonization after World War Two, elitist movements of protest took the form of political parties. The best known example of this was the Nigerian National Democratic Party formed in 1923. While protesting a strong desire to remain under British rule, this party, led by its founder and dominant leader, Herbert Macauley, sought better conditions for Nigerians in the colonial system like improved education and fair trading practices. It also fought elections to the limited membership afforded to Africans in the Lagos Legislative Council. But this was still an elitist movement, working within the confines of what was considered 'legitimate' by the colonial rulers, and addressing primarily those issues more beneficial to people of their own class.

More pervasive among the elite were the welfare associations more noticeable in East and Central Africa. They initially took the form of voluntary organizations of people with like interests. They were committed to improvements in education and religion or sought voting rights for taxpayers. There was a longer history of such organizations in some colonies than in others, depending on their colonial experience. In Nyasaland, for example, by 1912 a North Nyasa Native Association had been formed and in 1933 alone, fifteen such clubs were set up in the major cities. The Kikuyu Central Association formed in Kenya by the 1920s embraced members of a single ethnic group, but was very influential in the capital and in opposition to land alienation by the colonial rulers and the white settlers. Other welfare associations were set up in neighboring Northern Rhodesia, initially by migrants from Nyasaland which had a much earlier start with western education. In Southern Rhodesia, the Rhodesian Bantu Voters Association formed in 1923 was agitating for voting rights for Africans and the return of lands seized by the whites.

As colonial rule advanced, the African middle class became more informed about colonial policies and the strategies for combating unfavorable policies, while there was no let up on the abuses of the colonial system. This led Africans in these welfare associations to combine their efforts in amalgamating their groups to give them a stronger voice. In Northern Rhodesia, in response to the wishes of the white settlers to join with Southern Rhodesia as a hedge against possible African control, fourteen welfare associations were joined together in 1946 to form the federation of African Societies in Northern Rhodesia.

As these organizations consolidated, they were transformed into political movements, particularly after the Second World War. In Kenya, for instance, the Kikuyu Central Association and its affiliates were beginning to function as a political union after the Second World War as a response to the struggle over the land issue. Thus what had emerged as middle class movements seeking rights for a certain group, were basically the training ground for incipient nationalism as these became the basis for opposing the existence of colonial rule when the time was ripe. The amalgamated movements led to more aggressive, often violent protest as the groups found strength in numbers and as leadership increased with relatively expanded western education.

The West African Youth Movements

Another aspect of protest in British African colonies in West Africa was the Youth movements, involving basically young western trained Africans in the colonial capitals. These movements involved some political ambitions, essentially to take control of political agitation from the older, more conservative middle class. These youth movements also addressed primarily issues that could have benefited the urban bourgeoisie most, like improved wages, higher education provision and promotion into the upper rungs of the civil service.

The most radical of these movements that sought to involve the masses and attack the colonial system was started in Sierra Leone by Wallace Johnson. Though he was from Sierra Leone where the movement became best known, Wallace Johnson had been very influential in the organization of these movements both in Nigeria and the Gold Coast. He had been influenced by an International Labor Defence Congress he attended in

Moscow in 1932 and his activities consequently took on a strong working class and anti-colonial stance.

Wallace Johnson started operating as a journalist in Lagos, capital of Nigeria in 1931. In that same year, he organized an African Workers' Union in Nigeria. By 1932 he was editor of the Nigerian Daily Telegraph. His activism led in 1934 to the formation of the Nigerian Youth Movement (NYM) which included young intellectuals in Nigeria like Nnamdi Azikwe and Obafemi Awolowo, later to become very prominent in Nigerian politics. The NYM made at the time radical demands which included social welfare programs to benefit workers and the setting up of agricultural banks to modernize agriculture for the benefit of the peasants. While NYM agitation ultimately would include the masses, its program and activities, including a newspaper and petitions were still dominated by elite interests. But the NYM became a force in local politics in Nigeria, defeating the older Nigerian Democratic Party in the localized elections in Lagos in the 1930s. Apart from this the NYM achieved little else in the colonial system.

The elaborate youth movement activity in the Gold Coast and the zeal of its mover, J.B. Danquah seemed to have beckoned Wallace Johnson, for he moved to the Gold Coast when the colonial government started hounding him. Danquah had brought togethern a host of over fifty youth clubs and associations into a Youth Conference Movement which first met in Accra in 1929. In Accra, Wallace Johnson worked with Danquah in what became the West African Youth League (WAYL) with a strong workers' bias. The colonial government again sought Wallace Johnson out as a communist influenced agitator. He was convicted of seditious publication and expelled from the Gold Coast, finally settling in his native Sierra Leone in 1938.

In Sierra Leone, Wallace Johnson quickly set up his West African Youth League, agitating for workers' interests, leading to the formation of trade unions. His newspaper, the *African Standard*, was constantly exposing bad labor conditions and the poor educational system. Strikes erupted in mines and public employment areas as the WAYL expanded to a record membership of over forty thousand both in the capital, Freetown and in the interior. The colonial authorities at first tried unsuccessfully to use legal methods to silence Wallace Johnson. The start of the Second World War however provided an excuse for the colonialists to invoke extra-legal powers to detain Wallace Johnson. The WAYL therefore languished as Wallace Johnson was kept in detention for over four years

Youth movements in West Africa, particularly influenced by Wallace Johnson, remained a strong element of protest against colonial rule. They did not secure striking successes in changing colonial policies particularly because the political climate was not favorable for their advocacy. They however did provide a training ground for political leadership in the period after 1945 when the climate was more acceptable of such activity.

The Negritude Movement

Protests against colonial rule did not always take the form of agitation for amendment or removal of some debasing policy like the *indigenat* whose elimination leading Africans in the French African colonies fought desperately for. It sometimes took the form of a rejection of aspects of western culture as it was presented to Africans. Some of this development involved a transformation of some of the elements of western culture, like Christianity, into a more acceptable, Africanized form and this amounted to a denial of the colonialist conspiracy to present Christianity and western culture as inseparable.

A development similarly rejecting the colonialist assumptions that advancement meant westernization was the negritude movement among French African colonial subjects. This movement which developed in France itself was not confined to continental Africans. Diaspora Africans in French colonies in the Carribean Islands were also involved. In fact the first person to use the term negritude was Aime Césaire, a West Indian of African descent from the island of Martinique.

The negritude movement involved black subjects from French colonies who had initially become wedded to French culture and the philosophy of assimilation practiced in the French colonies. As already discussed in chapter three, this policy of assimilation meant a total disregard for any aspect of African culture as a basis for becoming qualified for French citizenship. Africans in the West Indian islands and on the continent had accepted this policy, some embracing it warmly. Many of them in the nineteenth and early twentieth century had found their way to Paris as was the trend for Africans seeking higher education to gravitate to the metropolitan capital of the colonizing power.

While in Paris, these Africans realized that the assumptions of assimilation, to become French citizens and be consequently equal to their white French counterparts, were not being fulfilled. They were subject to discrimination in virtually every aspect of society in France. This created a certain disillusionment. Some of these blacks in France became so despondent about abandoning their cultures that they determined to return to their African cultural roots. Thus the negritude movement involved a pronouncement and revival of African culture among Africans who had been led to forsake it. Obviously this developed in a very rarefied atmosphere in Paris, where the predominant attitude was racist and many of the Africans working there could hardly appreciate this new emphasis. The movement was expressed primarily in literary writings, but also in an appreciation of aspects of African culture. It therefore came to embrace a broader African cultural nationalism.

One leading light in the negritude movement was Leopold Sedar Senghor from Senegal, a highly educated intellectual who had taught at the Sorbonne in France. Senghor eventually got into politics to become the first President of Senegal. People like Senghor were handicapped by their removal from their African roots at an early age and therefore they had a more hazy familiarity with that culture. This sometimes meant a dependence on early European anthropological interpretations of African culture. Despite this handicap, negritude became very influential among educated Africans in the French colonies and among African diaspora intellectuals, particularly in the United States in the late 1960s and the 1970s

Conclusion

Protest movements in the colonial period in Africa therefore took a variety of forms, some more cultural like those related to Christianity and the negritude movement. Others like trade unions and youth movements were more abrasive and attacked more directly major pillars of the colonial hegemony. Depending on the degree of threat evinced by the colonial rulers, they tolerated or moved against these organizations with varying degrees of intensity and force. All of these movements however kept the element of alien rule alive among conquered Africans and also provided in many instances some training for the assumption of political activity, leading to the ending of colonial rule.

Questions

1. How significant were youth movements in protest against colonial rule in West Africa?
2. Christianity provided an important avenue of protest. Why do you think this was attractive to Africans?

Chapter VIII

ഌൟ

Transition in South Africa in the Twentieth Century

It is necessary to devote a special place to South African history in the twentieth century because of the influence it had on much of southern Africa and the rather peculiar development of racism in apartheid which attracted much international attention.

Minerals Affecting Political and Economic Change

By 1870, extensive diamond deposits were discovered in large areas around the Orange Free State, one of the Boer republics in the interior that emerged following the Great Trek. Claims to these diamond fields were made by the other Boer republic, the Transvaal (also called the South African Republic), by the Orange Free State and by African rulers in the area. Some of these black African rulers, particularly Waterboer who led the Griqua people, had the support of colored lawyers who advanced their claims.

These Boer republics were still independent entities as were the black African political units in the area. The Cape Colony, which was still under the British, was pressing for responsible government, a form of autonomy from Britain, which she received in 1872. This meant control of her own internal affairs and an increase in white racist policies as the Cape parliament was overwhelmingly dominated by the white minority. All of these white dominated governments in the region had interest in the diamond mines and so did the British. The British Governor at the Cape, Barkly, therefore maneuvered to establish a British protectorate over the area claimed by Waterboer and called it Griqualand West. This of course enraged the Boer republics.

The now self-governing Cape Colony government had no interest in supervising this new protectorate on Britain's behalf. The British government therefore developed the idea of federating all of the white and black African republics and kingdoms into one grand southern African colony under Britain. This way, Britain would have control over all of the mining areas.

Mining of diamonds and later gold created major changes in the economy of the region. Resources from mining transformed the economy from an agricultural to a mining and industrial one. The mining boom led to a burst of growth in railway construction to link up these areas so vastly apart and ease the movement of supplies and people. Whites and some blacks were drawn into mining which quickly became the greatest employer of labor. A shortage of labor resulted as mines and agriculture competed for workers, especially as the black independent farmers were not particularly willing to become wage laborers. The area around these mines therefore began exerting a strong pull for labor on the entire southern African region even as, with colonial rule, many Africans in southern Africa were increasingly squeezed from their land.

Thus all of the independent entities, white or black, were intent on using their independence to advantage in the trade and economic changes that accompanied mining. The British however forged ahead with the idea of controlling the entire region in one huge federation. Britain therefore schemed to establish control of the Transvaal which she annexed in 1877. This move was opposed by the Boers in the Transvaal itself, the Orange Free State and even those at the Cape.

In order to make this annexation more palatable to the Boers, the British proceeded to defeat African kingdoms in the interior that were deemed to be threats to the Boers. This, it was calculated, would at once extend British control in the area as well as appease the Boers. Thus the Pedi people were defeated by a British led force in 1879. The most powerful African kingdom in the area, the Zulu, was also attacked by a large British force on a trumped up charge. The Zulu gave a humiliating defeat to the British force at the Battle of Isandhlwana in early 1879. But the British sent another army later which defeated the Zulu. These attacks, together with those waged on the

Xhosa by the Cape Colony with British support, and by the Boer republics on smaller African kingdoms, soon brought to an end the era of independent African kingdoms in the region of South Africa by the end of the nineteenth century. The defeat of the Cape Colony forces by the Sotho kingdom led the Cape to abandon its role of controlling the distant interior. The Sotho kingdom thus passed to Britain and remained a separate British colony of Basutoland since 1884.

The opposition of the Boers to British control was sustained as the British suffered reverses at Isandhlwana and the Cape Colony government refused to cooperate with Britain over the federation idea. All of these factors encouraged the Transvaal Boers to rebel against British rule in 1880 and they scored a decisive defeat of British forces at Majuba Hill in 1881. Britain negotiated withdrawal and gave the Transvaal full internal self government.

Cecil Rhodes

By the mid 1880s then, it seemed that the British policy of controlling this rich diamond and gold areas under one federated colony had failed. It was around this time that Cecil Rhodes, a young British immigrant to South Africa, entered the picture. His career in the diamond mining industry moved very rapidly as he bought up most small mining concerns. Finally, he leveraged power in Britain to buy up the most powerful competitor, Barney Bernato, and set up the De Beers Consolidated Mines Ltd by 1888. This company came to dominate the world market in diamonds. Rhodes also bought a stake in gold mining with his consolidated Gold Fields of South Africa Limited.

Rhodes' mining organization was to contribute to a near complete subjugation of African labor and prevention of industrial action by a virtual imprisonment of the workers in camps. His greatest ambition however was to use his wealth to take control of the entire continent of Africa from the Cape to Cairo in Egypt on behalf of Britain. He entered into politics at the Cape Colony parliament in 1880.

The mid 1880s was the period of the intense scramble for Africa. The Germans had established themselves at South West Africa, next door to the Transvaal. The British in response therefore pushed inland to stake claim over Natal, Bechuanaland and Swaziland. The Cape Colony government was similarly establishing presence in the interior by annexing Gcalekaland and Thembuland, two African kingdoms.

It was around this time too, in 1886, that extensive deposits of gold were uncovered on the Rand around Johannesburg. This was in the Transvaal and it considerably boosted the Transvaal's desire and ability to maintain its independence and advance its economic development. This new wealth and desire for independence ran counter to British interest to control the region of South Africa and its new wealth at the height of the scramble for Africa. This was to provide the background to the Anglo-Boer war of 1899.

Background to the Anglo-Boer War of 1899

Rhodes became Prime Minister at the Cape Colony in 1890. He was responsible for some racist legislation in his short tenure, like the Glen Grey Act of 1894. This act abolished communal land ownership and restricted individual access to land. By restricting land holding among blacks to no more than a ten acre lot, the act ensured that no African landholder would become independent enough as a farmer without having to sell his labor. Thus the act accelerated the proleterianization of African labor. Rhodes also saw through the Franchise and Ballot Bill of 1892 which manipulated income and educational qualification for voter eligibility, intended to remove most Africans from the vote in the Cape Colony.

With this powerful position of Prime Minister backed by his wealth, Rhodes decided to push ahead with a plan to acquire territory in present day Zimbabwe and neighboring regions. It was understood that Zimbabwe had gold deposits, believed larger than the Rand. This new wealth Rhodes anticipated would reduce the Transvaal's economic importance. Add to this British control of territory north of the Transvaal, then the latter would be forced into a subordinate relationship with the British as a colony.

Rhodes planned to gain control of what became Northern Rhodesia, Malawi and Southern Rhodesia, all north of the Transvaal. He succeeded in doing this by every chicanery and deceit. The Matabele kingdom in Zimbabwe was conquered largely with the aid of the maxim gun and white volunteers from the Cape Colony who had been promised land and captured cattle. But the anticipated new wealth did not materialize as expected so Rhodes decided on a scheme to overthrow the Transvaal government. The plan involved encouraging the *uitlanders*, foreign miners, largely British, to stage an armed rebellion against the Transvaal government. A British police force set up by Rhodes would then travel to Johannesburg, the Transvaal capital, on a pretext of preserving order. The Transvaal would then be taken over for Britain. The plan failed as there was no armed rebellion by the *uitlanders*. The British position in the region was weakened while Rhodes was disgraced and forced to resign as Prime Minister at the Cape Colony.

The British did not however give up her intention of controlling the Transvaal and this was eventually to lead to war. The Transvaal ruler, Kruger, had come off strong from the botched raid planned by Rhodes and started arming his republic through the Germans in neighboring South West Africa. A mutual defense treaty with the Boers of the Orange Free State was strengthened. The British High Commissioner at the Cape, Milner, adopted an uncompromising stance in negotiation with Kruger, destroying all possibility of an agreement and enhancing Kruger's position in the eyes of Boers all over South Africa and even with moderate whites loyal to Britain. To pre-empt Britain, the Transvaal inevitably declared war in October 1899. Massive British forces were brought in to offset initial Boer victories. The Boers resorted to guerilla warfare and the British reacted by burning down Boer settlements and herding their women into unsanitary concentration camps. This only won more sympathy for the Boers, even in Britain, ascertaining that the peace treaty which followed would be favorable to the Boers.

Negotiations Following Peace and the Black Population

Though the Boers lost their independence as Britain won the war, the British agreed in the peace treaty that the question of a franchise for the Africans would not be raised before internal self-government had been given back to the former Boer republics. Thus Britain finally abandoned any responsibility for the African population and set the stage for the complete disenfranchisement of all non-whites in South Africa. In fact the British helped the Boers to re-establish their domination over the land and labor of the African population when these same Africans had assisted the British in the war against the Boers. In the years immediately following the war, Africans were dispossessed in the Boer republics as well as in Natal, another white dominated British colony in the South African interior, which had been given internal self-government in 1896. Successive rebellions by the Africans, like the 1903 rebellions against the poll tax and the Bambatha rebellion, were ruthlessly suppressed. African economic independence as small scale farmers was thus broken and they were transformed to wage laborers on mines and on white plantations.

Creation of the Union

Meanwhile, the British government was at last in a position to achieve a union of the various white settlements in South Africa. After drafting constitutions ensuring that there would be a unitary rather than a federal system in South Africa, the drafts were approved by the former Orange Free State, the Transvaal and Natal in 1909. The British government ratified the Union agreement in 1910 bringing about the Union of South Africa.

The union agreement gave higher proportional representation to the thinly white populated countryside as against the densely settled towns. This was a concession to the Boers who mostly lived outside the towns. All representation to the Union parliament was to be by whites only. The new constitution entrenched the votes of Africans and coloreds only at the Cape where they had had the franchise before. Africans were therefore barred from the electorate all over South Africa outside the Cape and the British government did nothing to change this.

The Drive towards Apartheid

The prosperity of white dominated South Africa depended on cheap labor. Every measure was therefore taken to ensure this. As Africans lost their land and economic independence, many were herded into reservations creating pools of cheap labor. It became in the interest of the whites to maintain the reservations and allow the Africans to migrate without their families to work in the mines and cities. That way, the African workers would not have their families to care for from the meager salaries. The rest of the families in the reservations would fend for themselves and would be more readily controlled in a restricted area. This encouraged a policy of segregation which successive South African governments pursued vigorously since the end of the nineteenth century. While there were often disagreements and incompatible interests between the mainly urban, business oriented British whites and the more rural Boers, they were all agreed on one issue. Africans should be kept under control as a reservoir of cheap labor. This factor dominated the progress towards apartheid.

The Native Land Act of 1913

Racist legislation had started under more moderate governments since the Union. The most important of these early legislation was the Native Land

Act of 1913. This was intended to prevent Africans from remaining as independent farmers with control over land outside the reserves. By the 1913 Land Act, Africans could no longer buy or lease land anywhere in South Africa except in the reservations. It also ended the practice of Africans farming on white owned land. The implication of this Act in the Cape was delayed because it would have meant existing land owners losing their land and consequently their vote, an issue entrenched in the constitution. This Act provided the basis of apartheid, the separating of the country into areas of black and white land ownership with the blacks deprived of access to fertile land they formerly owned. Later acts would only improve on this.

Another important piece of racist legislation in this early life of the union was the Urban Areas Act of 1923. This again was to determine that Africans could not permanently settle in the towns except they were working there. The basis of residential segregation was thus established by this law and together with the Native Land Act, laid the basis for racial segregation.

Politics after the union saw attempts to bring Boers and other whites into a single system in the South African National Party (SANP). This did not work. The Boers wanted dominance and Hertzog, a minister in the SANP played on this sentiment to break away from the SANP in 1914 and set up the National Party which was exclusively Boer. The South African Party, as the rump of the SANP became known, still controlled the government as the National Party continued to increase its popularity among the Boers.

Early Black Protest in the Union

African protest against these developments had continued throughout the Union. It had started in Ethiopian Christian movement which amounted to breakaway Churches that still retained western Christian interpretation of the religion. Examples like the Tembu Church and Nehemia Tile's breakaway from the Wesleyan Mission Church in 1884 marked the beginning of a movement that became influential all over southern Africa. A number of the middle class type organization were also formed and some like the African Peoples Organization (APO) sent a delegation to London to protest the unfavorable franchise proposals in the Union agreement. These groupings were more marked at the Cape where there was a colored and African bourgeoisie with rights to vote and own property. Newspapers were also printed by these elements like the *Imvo Zabantsundu* and the *Ilanga Lase Natal* in Natal. Many of these elite organizations, protesting primarily for benefits like a qualified franchise and property ownership for their own ranks, came together in 1912 to form a South African Native National Congress which was later renamed the African National Congress (ANC).

While the ANC was initially a bourgeois party, it sometimes espoused causes for the benefit of all black peoples. The two most prominent instances at this early stage were its support for the 1919 African mine workers strikes. As wages of white workers rose and repressive policies of the government, including pass laws, became evident, Africans were emboldened to strike for better wages. This was particularly so as white workers had struck in 1913 in the Rand and Natal. Protests against the pass system were launched by the ANC in Transvaal in 1919 and mine workers struck there later that year, supported by the ANC. Related clashes occurred between ANC supporters and white civilians and the strikes, though peaceful, were put down with much brutality by the South African government police.

The ANC was however still a peaceful organization and the strikes and pass action were an aberration. The ANC soon returned to its old pattern of paper and delegation protests. It was the Industrial and Commercial Workers Union (ICU) that came to take up workers' grievances. This Union was founded in 1914 by Klemens Kadalie and by December of that year it took part in organizing a strike of 400 dock workers in Cape Town. In 1928, the ICU held a day of formal protest against segregation laws and in 1929, the ICU in Natal was involved in a beer hall boycott which led a white mob to storm ICU offices. This provoked a riot in which six Africans and two whites were killed. Apart from these three moves the ICU went little further. Rent by its own moderation and dissention among its leadership and infiltrated by the South African government, the ICU virtually collapsed by the end of 1928.

The strikes and pass protest had been largely peaceful because of the strong influence of Indian protest in Natal led by Mahatma Gandhi, a young Indian lawyer returning home to India via South Africa after studies in Britain. Indians were equally discriminated against like Africans in all of the Union. Gandhi organized the movement called **satyagraha** in which the Indians destroyed their passes, courting arrest. Thousands were arrested and jailed until the government was forced to realize the futility of the arrests and decided to negotiate with Gandhi.

Gradual Assumption of Power by Afrikaner Nationalists

As labor conditions tightened with the recession following the Second World War, many white Boer workers were thrown out of employment. Many flocked to the towns where they had few usable skills and would not do the manual jobs for which blacks were very poorly paid. Violent protests and strikes by the white workers achieved little to change the condition of the white workers. The Labor Party which represented white workers decided on political action by forming an alliance with the Boer controlled National Party. This coalition to defend white Boer interest against the predominantly British controlled capitalist system in South Africa, won elections in 1924 and again in 1929.

This put the Boers in control and resulted in further racist legislation in favor of white interest. A Mines and Workers Amendment Act of 1926 excluded Africans and Asians from all skilled work while by an Immorality Act of 1927 sexual intercourse between whites and Africans became a criminal offence. The coalition attempted more extremist legislation, particularly aimed at destroying the African franchise at the Cape, but failed to secure the two-thirds majority to remove this entrenched clause from the constitution. The coalition leader, Hertzog, did however secure independence for South Africa from Britain by the Statute of Westminister in 1931. Although Boer nationalism increased under Hertzog, the extremist Boers were still not in full control. However, with the depression of the 1920s, their National Party merged with the South African Party to become the United Party.

The United Party won elections in 1933 and this gave Hertzog the majority needed to remove the Africans from the franchise at the Cape by the Native Representation Act of 1936. Hertzog refused to support Britain in the Second World War and lost popularity over this. His segment of the United Party was defeated and he ceased being Prime Minister. Boer nationalism had however grown by leaps and bounds. It had been influenced by Nazi type propaganda during the war and was staunchly supported by the Dutch Reformed Church which interpreted Christianity as a means of suppressing the Black population. Above all it was supported by the Broederbond, a secret organization of the Boers. The Broederbond became an instrument, like the Ku Klux Klan in the United States, for suppressing blacks with extra legal and violent methods. It was the Broederbond which orchestrated the adoption of Afrikaans, hitherto regarded as a pidginized version of Dutch, as the language of the Boers and from this the Boers increasingly became known as Afrikaners, to emphasize their separate identity.

As this gained ground, the Afrikaner nationalists exploited every opportunity to present the link with Britain and English speaking whites as oppression. The issue of South West Africa, a United Nations trust territory supervised by South Africa, is a case in point. When the United Nations, with strong Indian agitation, failed to approve the incorporation of South West Africa into the Union of South Africa, the Afrikaner nationalists capitalized on this as humiliation at the hand of a third world nation. They whipped up a black scare by accusing the United Party of opposing white interest by not taking a tough stand against Africans in the towns and in skilled employment. The increased white support resulting from this became advantageous as the Afrikaners had succeeded in weighting electoral seats in favor of rural, predominantly Afrikaner constituencies. These factors made it possible for the extremist National Party to win elections in 1948 by a slender majority of five seats.

The Setting Up of Apartheid

The new government under Dr. Malan then proceeded to systematize segregation following principles of apartheid. It entrenched Afrikaner rule by a number of devices. At the same time as the economy grew with mining and manufacturing based on African labor kept extremely cheap, explicit racist theories and attitudes were used to rigidly separate whites from non-whites in South Africa. This of course meant that Africans were banished to the reserves under what Afrikaners called responsible government, but ultimately under white control. Discriminatory laws were passed favoring Afrikaners in every aspect of society. This united even the poor Afrikaners behind the ruling establishment.

Africans were more firmly herded into reservations as their existing property rights, as well as those of colored peoples, were destroyed by laws like the Native Resettlement Act of 1956. African movement into towns was rigorously controlled by pass laws, infringement of which was also used as reason to jail Africans and use these prisoners as cheap farm labor. Laws prevented Africans from holding industrial action. All institutions including trade unions, were rigidly segregated by law. Marriages and sex between whites and blacks became criminal offences. Education was segregated especially by the Bantu Education Act of 1953 which provided separate and inferior education for Africans. African education was now controlled by the Native Affairs Department, not the Department of Education. A series of moves, including as well packing the parliament, enabled the government to eliminate the entrenched clause in the constitution and remove the Cape Colored from the regular franchise in the 1950s.

As even some liberal whites opposed the extremist policies, the Afrikaner government passed the Suppression of Communism Act in 1953 which banned the Communist Party as well as set up a broad interpretation of communism which could be used to silence all opposition to the government.

Opposition to Apartheid

There were some liberal white organizations protesting apartheid and seeking an ideal multi racial society. An example of this was the Liberal Party formed in 1953. Such movements were invariably not seriously concerned with the rights of non-whites and some never even would allow non-whites to become members. The Liberal Party, however, attempted a multi racial membership. It had little support from white voters and was harassed by the government until legislation was passed banning multi racial parties.

Much of the overt opposition to apartheid came from black movements. As blacks grew more desperate and despaired at all forms of discrimination, they became bolder in organizing opposition even against the apartheid government's harsh laws forbidding such protests.

Opposition from a Reorganized ANC

The ANC had seen some reorganization by 1940 under Dr. Xuma, with a youth wing of young teachers and students of medicine and law. These latter, though still attached to the earlier ideals of the ANC leaders, were advocating for massive passive resistance action to achieve their aims. Workers' protests had continued throughout the 1940s, like the African Mine Workers Union strike in 1946, especially at the Rand and the Village Deep Mine where police opened fire on workers who were resisting being forced back to work. The ANC was now beginning to assume a position championing such moves.

The ANC cooperated with the South African Indian Congress, overcoming earlier differences between blacks and Indians and by 1952 they together launched an organized campaign of civil disobedience to court arrest from the government. The plan gathered initial momentum but the government responded by massive arrests. Spontaneous rioting broke out in several areas after these arrests and the government quelled the uprisings with much savagery. This endeared the government to the whites and contributed to its winning the 1953 elections.

The ANC and the Freedom Charter

The ANC again reorganized after its leader, Dr. Moroka lost credibility. A new leader, Albert Luthuli, was appointed in 1953 and at the ANC conference in December of that year, a new initiative came forward. This was to be a huge rally of all non-white organizations and peoples to define a charter of liberties. This gave rise to the Congress of the People in 1955 that issued the Freedom Charter. The Charter elaborated their vision of a just South Africa with equality for all races, redistribution of land and nationalization of industries.

The Afrikaner government reacted months later in 1956 by searching the houses of all leaders who were promptly arrested and charged with treason. Though these were acquitted in November 1961 after mammoth trials, they had been kept incarcerated for so long, depriving their organizations of leadership and demonstrating the government's heavy handedness. Leadership aside, protests continued throughout the late 1950s. There was for example rioting among the Pedi people in northern Transvaal in 1958. A prolonged boycott of municipal buses also took place in Johannesburg in 1959 as well as a riot sparked off by a police liquor raid in Durban township in which nine policemen were killed.

The Pan African Congress
and the Sharpeville Massacre

In March 1958, younger militants of the ANC led by Robert Sobukwe who were disillusioned by cooperation between the ANC and liberal white organizations, walked out of the Transvaal ANC meeting and subsequently formed the Pan African Congress (PAC) in 1959. The PAC rejected cooperation with other race groups though its ultimate goal was a multi racial South Africa.

Competition ensued between the ANC and PAC for leadership of black protest. When the ANC annual Congress met in December 1959, it decided on a mass anti-pass campaign scheduled for March 31, 1960. The PAC then announced a similar campaign for ten days earlier than that of the ANC. The PAC campaign was supported by the ANC. Sobukwe deliberately broke pass laws and was arrested. Crowds gathered outside a police station in the township of Sharpeville and the police then opened fire on the crowd, continuing to fire on the fleeing crowd. Sixty-nine people were reported killed and 180 wounded. The Sharpeville Massacre, as it came to be known, aroused international opinion against apartheid as graphic images of this were brought to western television screens. Luthuli identified with the PAC move by publicly burning his own pass-book a few days later and called for a national stay at home day for those killed.

The South African government responded with a series of police raids. Over 1800 people were arrested. Rioting broke out in a number of centers, some led by the PAC in Cape Town and Durban. The government declared a state of emergency, meaning a suspension or regular legal processes, and declared the ANC and PAC illegal organizations.

In 1961, Nelson Mandela and other former ANC leaders called on the government to effect a meeting of all races to work out a new constitution or face a national strike. The government rejected this outright whereupon Mandela and others went underground. A militant wing of the ANC was then formed, called *Umkhonto we sizwe* (spear of the nation. Its aim was selective sabotage to material installations. The PAC also formed a similar organization called *Poqo* dedicated to guerilla warfare.

In reaction to criticism after Sharpeville and the armed struggle launched by the black organizations, the South African police were given wider powers of search, detention and suppression which only further eroded black rights. Under these extended powers, Mandela, the leader of *umkhonto we sizwe*, was captured at a farm near Rivonnia in 1963. He was tried and sentenced to life imprisonment in 1964. This did not kill opposition. In 1969, a new nationalist movement inspired by the black power movement in the United States emerged among black students in South Africa. Black Students broke away from the multi racial National Union of South African Students and formed the South African Student Organization (SASO) led by Steve Biko. This came to spur the development of a wider Black People's Convention. The black consciousness movement, as it was called, rejected cooperation with white movements, seeking to harmonize anti-white opposition among blacks, colored and Indian groups. Steve Biko eventually died in prison from brain injuries due to police torture. With all this repression, many blacks began to go underground and leave South Africa to cross the borders and join the ANC cells developing in the neighboring newly independent African countries.

The Bantustans

Increased international attention and pressure led the South African government under J.B. Vorster to put forward its own version of response to black aspirations for political rights. This was the Promotion of Bantu

Self Government Act of 1959. This called for separate development for Africans in the reservations that were now re-labeled 'homelands.' Deriving from the word Bantu which white South Africans used to refer to all South African blacks, the *Bantustans* were supposed to provide responsible government for blacks in the barren reservations. The first *bantustans* to be granted "independence" under this law was the Transkei in 1963. Years later in the 1970s, some eight other *bantustans* were granted homeland status. It was clear that these were artificial enclaves, dependent on the South African government which controlled and funded them. This control amounted to appointing or removing officials in the *bantustans*. Land allocated to each *bantustan* was inadequate to hold the population for which it was intended.

Changing Circumstances in Southern Africa

The situation in southern Africa which had been favorable to the South African government's apartheid policy began to change radically in the 1970s. South Africa had been shielded throughout the 1960s by the neighboring Portuguese colonies of Angola and Mozambique where Portugal was faced with massive revolutionary wars in response to its refusal to grant any kinds of concessions to its African subjects. South Africa had cooperated with Portugal against the guerilla fighters and this helped South Africa in clamping down on dissidence in neighboring Namibia, dominated by South Africa which abused its United Nations mandate.

In 1974 the Portuguese army, exhausted by the colonial war, overthrew the government of the dictator, Caetana who had succeeded Salazar. The immediate result of this revolution was the signing of agreements with the liberation movements in Mozambique and Angola that same year to grant them independence in 1975. Oil and diamond rich Angola was however a big prize not to be let go of that easily. With outside support, factions developed in Angola which brought a continuing civil war to Angola. The main faction holding the capital, Luanda, and surrounding areas was led by a marxist oriented government, the *Movimento Popular de Libertação de Angola* (MPLA). To the north, another movement, the *Frente Nacional de Libertação de Angola* (FNLA), was supported by the U.S and the neighboring leader of Zaire, Mobutu Sese Seko. To the south, a third group, *União Nacional para a Independencia Total de Angola* (UNITA), was propped up by South Africa which sent troops to fight against the Marxist government at the capital. The MPLA received help from communist countries, especially Cuban troops sent to Angola which helped the MPLA to quickly defeat the FNLA. With the civil war in Angola being interpreted as part of the cold war between the east and the west, American support was later shifted to back UNITA against the MPLA. Thus South Africa's support for UNITA was being seen as anti-communist. South Africa's intention was clearly to create as much instability in Angola and other neighboring African states as possible. This they believed would prevent these states from uniting against South Africa or helping the ANC fighters or those of the South West African Peoples Organization (SWAPO), the liberation movement in South West Africa which also was fighting against the South African government. By the early 1980s, South African troops were invading and occupying parts of Angola, thus further complicating that country's civil war.

These developments meant that South Africa no longer had friends along its northern borders. This position was further worsened by the rebellion against white minority rule in Southern Rhodesia and the progress being made by the guerilla army there. Areas liberated by the rebels in Southern Rhodesia were sufficient ground for the ANC to execute planning activity against South Africa. In fact the Rhodesian rebels won the war against white minority rule and an African majority government emerged there as independent Zimbabwe in 1980. Added to the independence of all the other African states north of South Africa, a greater problem was created for the apartheid government.

Internal Developments and Protest

The problems for the white minority ruling South Africa were thus increased particularly as the ANC was stepping up its armed rebellion against the government, coming from the northern frontier. There were however more problems internally. As the economy began to demand more skilled labor with more permanent residency in the towns, the government and industry began to grudgingly respond to this, giving African workers a greater voice. This of course spurred the desire for more rights.

If the totality of police control could seriously impede adult protest, school children, who also felt all the pangs of apartheid, took up the gauntlet. In June 1976 in the township of Soweto, they broke out in mass protest against the imposed use of Afrikaans as the language of instruction in education. Mass riots, largely spontaneous, followed through into 1977 in different parts of South Africa and proved difficult for the police to quell, even with added heavy army gunfire. Large numbers of blacks were killed and arrested and many died in prison. Others fled to join the guerillas in neighboring African countries. A down side of this increased military activity for the South African government was that the army came to have a stronger role in government and began the inevitable task of courting black support in the army since there were not enough whites to serve as recruits.

Throughout the first part of the 1980s then, smoldering discontent continued as youths virtually took over the townships and enforced their own will, particularly against suspected black informants of the South African government. The government too was completely absorbed with controlling the violence in the townships, while vocal blacks like Archbishop Desmond Tutu and other white liberals began to make bold attacks on the system of apartheid. The government attempted to employ divide and rule tactics, giving more rights to coloreds and Indians and supporting organized black movements opposing the ANC like Chief Gatsha Buthelezi's Inkatha Freedom Party. The apartheid government also began making overtures to African governments north of South Africa in a bid to neutralize anti South African activity. The ANC operating from neighboring African countries was scoring increasing success in raising the level of fear among the white population by successful bombing of some installations in South Africa in 1980 and stepping up guerilla activity along South Africa's borders.

The Fall of Apartheid

By the mid 1980s, it was beginning to be accepted even by some of the most conservative of racist whites that at least some political accommodation of blacks was inevitable. There was increased pressure from all sides. International pressures from the United States, the British Commonwealth and the United Nations were leading to more effective sanctions which began to take a toll on the South African economy. Despite raids on its bases in Zambia, Botswana and Zimbabwe, the ANC was increasing in stature both in South Africa and internationally. The extended military activity to control violence among blacks in South Africa and to prosecute the war against the ANC and SWAPO guerilas was having an adverse effect on South Africa. Even as South Africa renewed its onslaught on Angola in support of UNITA and to deny SWAPO bases, the cold war was ending and both the United States and Soviet Union were sending signals of a withdrawal of interest in this region. Since South Africa could not effectively defeat the Cuban supported MPLA government in Angola, the United States and Soviet Union joined the United Nations in pressing South Africa to accept a peace agreement and withdraw from Angola and Namibia by 1989 and Namibia became independent in 1990.

Most factions in the apartheid government in South Africa were now pushing harder for an agreement with the ANC in the face of these developments. Though the ANC was not in a very advantageous position militarily, extensive violence was continuing in the townships. When the leader of the government, P.W. Botha temporarily relinquished office in June 1989, his successor F.W. de Klerk took a forward push in going to the Zambian capital to meet ANC leaders. As this was supported by most of the cabinet and members of both political parties, it ensured that de Klerk would be confirmed as head of government.

With this kind of support and continued threat of tougher sanctions from the United States and United Nations, de Klerk proceeded to release Nelson Mandela from prison and undo the ban on the ANC and all political movements in 1990. He announced negotiations towards universal suffrage, signaling black majority rule. The ANC agreed to abandon the armed struggle as amnesty was given to all returning exiles by 1991. Virtually all apartheid acts were repealed in 1991.

Much of the negotiations for a new constitution occurred against a background of continued civil war between supporters of Inkatha and the ANC. Inkatha was financially and materially supported by the white South African government and its forces, in an apparent bid to discredit blacks, particularly the ANC and put the latter at a disadvantage in the constitutional negotiations. In spite of this talks continued, agreement being finally reached for a government of national unity. Elections were fixed for 1994 and South Africa achieved majority rule following the elections with Mandela as the first black president.

Post Apartheid

While this marked the end of white minority political domination in South Africa, it did not end white control of the economy. Whites still owned an extremely disproportionately higher percentage of the best land in South Africa and controlled virtually all industries. The new government under Mandela found itself under extreme international warnings and pressure against disrupting the economy. It therefore found it difficult to make bold moves to affect white control of land, industry and even the press. Mandela increasingly kept quiet about earlier promises to address the question of redistribution of land. The new government did however set up a Truth and Reconciliation Commission to make public the crimes against humanity committed by particularly the white apartheid government. Reconciliation largely meant a public laundry of dastardly acts, supposedly enough to satisfy particularly black South Africans. Blacks in South Africa still live largely in poor townships, have less access to quality education and employment and the white economic establishment is trying hard to keep the status quo. Change from this situation will remain a very slow process.

In 1999, Nelson Mandela stepped down from office and was succeeded by Thaba Mbeki as the leader of the ANC and the new President of South Africa.

Questions

1. Give an explanation of some labor policies pursued by successive South African governments in the twentieth century which destroyed the economic independence of blacks in South Africa.
2. Evaluate the role of protest in bringing down apartheid in South Africa.

Chapter IX

ॐ

The Movement Towards African Decolonization

There were many political, economic and social changes in the African colonies by the end of the Second World War. These changes affected primarily the attitudes and determination of elements among the educated elite, urging them to press for more concessions from the colonial rulers. Some of these changes were influenced by earlier developments both within and without the African continent. Significantly also, one needs talk about a changing attitude among the colonial powers, particularly the British, and to a lesser degree the French, which resulted in political concessions to their African colonies. The changes conceded by the colonial rulers and demanded by the African leaders gathered momentum in this post Second World War period and were to lead to independence for most African colonies.

Influences from Outside the Continent—The Pan-African Movement

Some of the factors affecting political change in the colonies were related to events outside Africa. One of these was the movement to seek the welfare of people of African descent wherever they were found—in Europe, the Americas, the Carribean or on the continent of Africa itself. This movement affected the thinking of particularly Africans studying or living outside the continent, a number of whom were to return to their homelands and lead the movement towards self-rule. But this Pan-African development also had a more direct impact on those living in Africa itself and led to often swift reaction by the colonial rulers to suppress the movement.

Marcus Garvey and the United Negro Improvement Association (UNIA)

The Pan-African movement was not a coordinated movement even though some of the major actors related to each other at certain points in time. One important figure in the early stages of this movement was Marcus Garvey, the Jamaican born activists who agitated for Black people to look positively on their own heritage and capabilities and to return to Africa and build up the continent into a powerful force. Garvey had started the UNIA in Jamaica with little success but when he moved to New York City in 1917, his agitation and the UNIA scored quick success. Though he was opposed by upper class Blacks both in Africa and the United States, Garvey's slogans of 'Africa for the Africans,' 'Ethiopia Awake,' 'Back to Africa' and the Black Star (shipping) Line had an attractive ring to the masses of dispirited blacks in America. His movement became popular in New York and his newspaper, *The Negro World*, became a prominent organ, translated into Spanish and French. Garvey even called a Pan-African meeting in New York in 1920.

Garvey's UNIA and *Negro World* had a significant impact within Africa itself. UNIA branches were started in Nigeria, the Gold Coast and Sierra Leone. In Sierra Leone, a Garvey supporter named John Davies, proclaimed himself 'king and emperor of Africa,' issuing a public pronouncement in a circular tract in 1922 to give effect to Garvey's slogan of 'Africa for the Africans.' Davies in his tract ordered all imperialists out of Sierra Leone. The circular reached the Governor General of French West Africa who asked Governor Slater of Sierra Leone to look into the matter. French and British colonial officials began suppressing *The Negro World*. It became a crime punishable by imprisonment to be found in possession of any Garveyite publication.

In Liberia, which had been earmarked as Garvey's African empire base, the United States put pressure on the government which dissociated itself from the Garvey movement. Though Garvey was silenced by the United States government which jailed him in 1933 for misusing the US mail to collect funds for his movement, and then deported him in 1925, Garvey's movement had helped to stir the imagination of Africans both in Africa and the diaspora. Leaders of the independence movement like Kwame Nkrumah of Ghana would refer to the influence of Marcus Garvey and Nkrumah used Garvey's Black Star Line as an important symbol in independent Ghana.

The Pan-African Congresses

Another development which was to influence educated Africans in the struggle against colonial rule was a series of Pan African Congresses held in Europe and the United States throughout the first half of the twentieth century. The idea had actually started with a Chicago congress in 1893 in which leading American Blacks like Alexander Crummel and Bishop Henry Turner participated and Africans like Edward Blyden and Rev. James Johnson of Nigeria sent or promised papers for the meeting. This Pan African idea was further developed by Henry Sylvester Williams, an Afro West Indian barrister in London, when he formed the African Association of blacks interested in forging links towards a stronger voice on the problems of peoples of African descent. It was this group which largely supported another Pan African Congress in London in 1900. Apart from the representation of blacks living in England and the US, there were ten representatives from Africa, mostly from West Africa, but including an assistant to Emperor Menelik of Ethiopia. The meeting discussed issues of black empowerment and black history in general, but also condemned British policies concerning blacks in South Africa and the Rhodesias. The conference set up a secretariat with Sylvester Williams as secretary, and regional branches with W.E.B. Dubois, an African-American activist, in charge of the American branch.

The leading personality in the continuation of the Pan African ideal was to become W.E.B. Dubois. He organized another Pan African conference in Paris in 1919 to put the interest of African peoples to the attention of the world powers who were then meeting in Paris to hammer out a peace treaty following the First World War. Dubois was able to secure the cooperation of Blaise Diagne, the first African to be elected as a deputy or parliamentarian to the French Assembly. The conference therefore did not secure the participation of English speaking Africans. Two other such conferences, rather low key, were held in 1923 in London and in 1927 in New York.

The most important of these Pan African conferences was the one held in Manchester in 1945 and presided over by Dubois. The organizing committee for that conference had Kwame Nkrumah from the Gold Coast and George Padmore from the West Indies as Secretaries, while Jomo Kenyatta of Kenya was the Assistant Secretary. The conference hall was draped with the flags of independent black states of Liberia, Ethiopia and Haiti. Many of the Africans who were to become prominent in the anti-colonial struggle attended this meeting, including prominent names like Obafemi Awolowo of Nigeria, Dr. Hastings Banda of Malawi and I.T.A. Wallace Johnson of Sierra Leone. Many African organizations including trade unions in Africa, the ANC of South Africa and the UNIA in the US were all represented. Delegates from Africa were in full force for the first time in this kind of conference.

The conference discussed 'Imperialism in North and West Africa,' as well as problems in South and Central Africa, and Jomo Kenyatta presented on 'the East African Picture.' The conference called for 'complete and absolute independence' indicating that force may be necessary to achieve this, if the colonial powers were unwilling to grant it. This conference was therefore to have a profound impact on the Africans mentioned above, who returned to their home colonies to be in the forefront in the fight for independence in Africa.

The West African Students Union (WASU)

An equally important organization which linked up with the Pan African Conferences and Garveyism was the West African Students Union (WASU). It was formed in London in 1925 by a Nigerian law student, Ladipo Solanke, who had been active in pan-African movements in Britain. Solanke mobilized other Africans into reviving African protest against oppression and degradation. While the movement tended to cling to the idea of the emergence of a West African nation as a nucleus for a united Africa, it always embraced a pan-African accent. Thus, in spite of its 'West African' and 'student' designation, the movement included other non-West African, non-students like Jomo Kenyatta. When Garvey was released from prison in the US, he went to London to try and revive his UNIA in less auspicious circumstances. He provided one of the early secretarial centers for WASU.

Ladipo Solanke toured West Africa on behalf of the Union, opening branches led by former members who had returned to their native lands. Solanke also collected funds on this visit to open a hostel in England for Africans. Like the other movements, WASU became a source of agitation for African rights and published a magazine, *WASU*, which had a wide international circulation. WASU specifically addressed issues of nationhood for African colonies. Many who worked with the 1945 Pan African Conference were members of WASU which remained a source of influence on future African leaders.

Socio-Economic Changes

Developments that accompanied the Second World War brought changes in the perspective and fortunes of Africans, and this was to contribute in no small measure to a more accelerated push for freedom from colonial rule.

This Great War was to give a fillip to economic changes in African countries. Increased production to support the war effort became necessary. In the French colonies, as this government controlled production increased with forced labor, export was stifled by limitations imposed by inadequate transportation. It therefore became necessary to process some of this produce like groundnuts locally. Equally so, fear of enemy submarines limited imports to the colonies so that people had to depend on local production by blacksmiths and weavers. Thus in spite of hardship, the war led to a stimulation of economic activity in the colonies.

In the British colonies production of primary commodities like palm oil, rubber, tin and aluminum was intensified after the British lost to Japan her colonies in Burma and Malaya. The demand for these products became so acute that Britain too resorted to forced labor in tin mines in Nigeria. This contribution was then in addition to the virtually forced collection of monies by Africans to support the war effort. British dependence on these commodities again stimulated production and consequently increased demands on labor, with wage labor seeing an upward spiral. But also, as shipping space was limited to send these products to Europe, various secondary industries developed in the colonies, further stimulating economic activity.

The increased economic activity was also related to a need for improved infrastructure like better airports, roads and port facilities. All of these, necessary for the war effort, meant more jobs and income for the people in the colonies, even though much of the income was eaten up by inflation as particularly imported goods were very scarce.

In addition to these war induced economic factors, the British brought into operation the Colonial Development and Welfare Acts of 1940 for economic and social development in the colonies to stave off rebellions as had recently occurred in the West Indies. These funds were for building improved roads, schools and hospitals in the colonies. While these were meager amounts meant to be matched by funds from each colony, they provided an added source of economic stimulation in the colonies.

The French equivalent of this, the *Fonds d'investissement pour le développement économique et social* (FIDES) was actually directly related to the war. It was France's way of rewarding the colonies for their tremendous support on which France had depended to prosecute the war. The FIDES grants were generally much larger than the Colonial Development and Welfare funds provided by Britain.

Many of these economic changes induced widespread urbanization in the colonies as people moved to get the attendant jobs, even as a good segment of the labor force was recruited, often forcefully, to fight in the war.

Social Change

Economic and other changes occasioned by the war began to influence the African population in a variety of ways, increasing social tensions and affecting attitudes. For the first time, Africans came to see the vulnerability of the colonial masters who had set themselves up on a high pedestal. This considerably reduced the prestige of the white man which had been a important basis of upholding colonial rule. France was divided between the occupying forces and the Vichy Regime. Propaganda literature was flying back and forth between these two hostile factions and some of this attack literature called into question the validity of holding colonies. Africans in the French colonies were beginning to see this literature. Britain on the other hand was being defeated in East Asia by the Japanese whom the British considered inferior peoples.

More significantly, the interaction between working class black and white elements was bringing new visions to the Africans. White troops passing through West Africa interacted with African civilians and soldiers. These white soldiers would sometimes discuss common elements of oppression of those at the bottom of society, white or black. These arguments were never completely lost on the Africans, particularly when they came from other whites.

These exchanges were more significant among Africans who served in the war outside Africa. They saw service in Europe, North Africa, the Middle East, India and Burma. Africans from the colonies served besides white soldiers, ordinary citizens, sometimes more cowardly than themselves. Slowly they came to believe that the white man was ordinary flesh and blood like themselves, not the exalted superhuman lords they had been led to believe. As Africans served in places like India and Burma, they came to realize that the picture of degradation in their lives painted by colonial rule was no worse than existed in India and Burma. In India, some of the African soldiers came to learn that India's participation in the war on the side of the British had only been achieved as India extracted promises of independence from the British.

Many more African soldiers were able to appreciate these issues as even unlettered recruits had been taught to read and write in the army. Some were taught technical skills during their service which also helped to broaden their horizons.

As these African soldiers returned home after the war, they became part of the teeming, restive urban dwellers. Their improved knowledge about what happened elsewhere meant that few were willing to return to rural life. As the economies did not expand after the war, it meant that many of these returned soldiers did not receive employment that they considered they were entitled to, having fought for the colonial rulers in wars that had little to do with Africans. It was now readily possible for political leaders to enlist a large disaffected audience in the towns to listen to and support their anti-colonial calls. These were messages the soldiers could readily relate to, remembering their new experience from the war. They were also significant enough in numbers to reinforce similar messages with the rest of the urban population.

Other International Issues

World War II had other implications for spurring leading Africans to seek freedom from colonial rule. In defense of European interests during the war, the British Prime Minister, Winston Churchill and the U.S. President Franklin Roosevelt had both signed the Atlantic Charter as the US joined the war in 1941. The Charter had declared the freedom of people to choose the government under which they would live. This pronouncement was welcomed by leading Africans like those in WASU and also the king of Morocco who began to request its application to his territory.

In September 1941, one month after the signing of the Charter, Churchill was stating in the British parliament that the pronouncement of self-determination would be applied to the European peoples and not the British Empire that included the African colonies. But Roosevelt had no such double intentions. Coming from the US with a strong anti-colonial background,

Roosevelt kept pursuing the issue of the dismantling of the British Empire. In 1945, Roosevelt was supported by the Soviet leader, Stalin, in demanding the break-up of the British Empire.

While Soviet activities by 1948 ushered in the Cold War and diluted US criticism of Britain and her empire, the Soviet block remained a strong critic of empire. Soviet Marxist ideology of the eventual triumph of the working class over capitalism, had strong leanings with the idea of eliminating the suppression of the weak. Thus a strong anti-imperialist stance was supported by the communist doctrine signifying also the ultimate triumph of imperial subjects against colonialism. The Soviet Union therefore kept a continuous attack on the colonial powers at the United Nations, urging for independence for the colonial territories. Since the US did not particularly oppose this attack, the tirade had a large potential for embarrassing the colonial powers.

International pressures coming from these sources continued to place the issue of freedom for the colonies awkwardly in the face of the colonial powers and to encourage African leaders to press for freedom for their territories. The granting of independence to the British colonies of India and Pakistan in 1947 further raised the possibility of similar dispensation for other British colonies. By the end of the Second World War, particularly with the new Labor government in England, an atmosphere of willingness to make concessions to her colonies was evident with the British. The fact also that there were no colonies of white settlers in West Africa to raise objections made it easier to pursue those concessions particularly in West Africa.

The most important element in the drive towards independence however was the political movement that developed often with force in the individual colonies. This piled up the pressure on the British and French governments. The two most prominent of these movements were the Mau Mau rebellion in Kenya and the Algerian revolution, both running through the 1950s. The human and material cost of these rebellions to the colonial powers led them to finally conclude that it was necessary to grant independence to their colonies.

Questions

1. Discuss the economic and social changes brought about in the African colonies which stimulated the movement towards independence.
2. What role did organizations by people of African descent outside the continent play in the independence drive?

Chapter X

୫ଠ୯ଽ

The Struggle for Independence I: North Africa, the Horn, and the French African Colonies

The Algerian war and the Mau Mau movement were evidently the deciding factors in forcing the hand of the colonial rulers to grant independence to their colonies. There were however about the same time pro-independence political movements threatening disruption and rebellion in a number of colonies like the Gold Coast and later in Central African colonies like Northern Rhodesia. It should also be pointed out that by the end of the 1950s decade when some of these movements gathered steam, the British and French had finally decided to grant independence to their African empires. It became clear to the imperialists that the identification of pliable individuals who could be negotiated with and to whom power would be surrendered was better that managing costly rebellions. Essentially, it was evident that by this method the colonial rulers could retain control of their interests in these colonies, their policies being carried on by a colonial minded, westernized bourgeoisie. Let us look at these independence movements and the areas they developed in, starting with North Africa.

Egyptian Nationalism and Independence

The Algerian revolution can best be understood within the context of developments in North Africa in the twentieth century, particularly in Egypt. Strong support for the Algerian war from Egypt was significant to the success of the nationalists in Algeria.

Political agitation was a continuing phenomenon since the North African countries fell under colonial rule. France ruled Algeria after its seizure in 1830 and also ruled Morocco and Tunisia after declaring protectorates there in the late nineteenth century. Egypt was dominated by Britain after the invasion of 1882 and the declaration of a British protectorate there in 1914. The fundamental issue of a Christian English overlord over a zealous Islamic population never sat well with Egyptians. Agitations for independence after the First World War based on hopes raised by Woodrow Wilson's support for self determination had been met with repression and leading nationalists like Saad Zaghul had been exiled to France. Violence erupted in 1919 and following British fears for the worst, Britain decided to grant self government to Egypt in 1922, retaining control over foreign policy, defense, the Suez Canal and business interests. The traditional rule of the sultan was converted into a monarchy which never worked out well.

In 1936, the popular Wafd party came into office in Egypt. Its nationalist fervor threatened British control of Egypt. Added to this, Italy was mounting hostile anti-British propaganda in Ethiopia which she had conquered in 1935, and also in Egypt. Britain's response to this Italian and nationalist threat in Egypt was to sign a treaty with Egypt granting independence to that country in 1935. The treaty ended the system of *capitulations* imposed on Egypt by Britain, by which foreigners were not subject to Egyptian law and taxation. Britain however retained control by that treaty over important elements of Egyptian sovereignty, including a right to 'protect' the Suez Canal.

These aspects of control still exercised by Britain in Egypt only continued to fuel nationalist resentment, heightened also by Egypt's participation in the Second World War on the side of Britain. Nationalist pressure therefore moved the Wafd government in 1945 to press for negotiations with the British to amend the 1936 treaty in favor of Egypt. The talks however broke off amid mass demonstrations in Cairo, the Egyptian capital in 1947. Egypt took the matter to the newly formed United Nations but failed to gain support.

The Egyptian nationalist agitation soon became embroiled in a larger international problem involving the Arab world as Egypt, like most of the North African countries, was predominantly peopled by Arabs. Britain had supported Egypt's prominent role in the creation of the Arab League which included Arabs in North Africa and the Middle Eastern countries. Britain and the US at the end of the War imposed the creation of the state of Israel in Palestinian territory in the heart of the Arab world. This development led to war between the Arabs and Israel which was backed by Britain, France and the United States. The Arab League of course lost the war against Israel and demonstrations broke out in Cairo to oppose both the failure of the Egyptian government in that war and Britain's continued domination of Egypt.

Virtual anarchy broke out in Egypt as the newly re-elected Wafd government lost control of the economy and popular discontent. These pressures pushed the government into a firmer stance in negotiations with Britain, leading to a unilateral renunciation by Egypt of the 1936 treaty. This did not save the day as the Wafd government fell amid rioting in Cairo in 1952. It was military officers who finally gained control of the situation. The king Farouk was forced to abdicate, ending the monarchy in 1953. By then a Revolutionary Council of the military had assumed control with General Neguib as President. Ultimately, it was the more radical Gamel Abd el-Nasser who became head of state in 1954.

Nasser was now trying to build up his military but he could not get arms supply from the west. He then turned to Czechoslovakia and Eastern European countries. This decision in the middle of the cold war enraged the western countries. Britain, the United States and the World Bank retaliated by refusing to finance the Aswan High Dam in Egypt that was intended to address Egypt's economic problems. Nasser replied by nationalizing the Suez Canal Company in 1956. Proceeds from this company, Nasser announced, would be used to finance the Aswan Dam. The western press launched a massive campaign against Egypt, deceiving their own public by stating that Nasser had blocked international use of the Suez Canal by nationalizing the Canal, which had always been part of Egypt.

When pressures failed to get Nasser to relent, Britain, France and Israel launched a military attack on Egypt that same year, calculated to reduce Egypt again to a colony. As Isreali troops invaded Egypt and the French and British mounted air attacks, the US and Soviet Union began to call for a ceasefire in the United Nations. Pressures from these super powers succeeded in getting the Isreali forces to pull back. This prevented Britain and France from taking over Egypt. The 1956 war however elevated Nasser in the eyes of third world nations and colonial peoples as one who would stand up against European imperialism.

The Algerian Revolution—
Growth of Nationalist Pressures

Like Egypt, the predominantly Muslim population in Algeria continued to be opposed to domination by Christian rulers, the French, ever since French colonization in 1830. Opposition had however mainstreamed by the early twentieth century in the pattern of bourgeois politics acceptable to the French.

There was one particular difference in Algeria. By the 1940s there were close to one million French settlers in Algeria. Referred to as the *pieds noirs* (black legs), these settlers dominated the politics and economy in this French colony. They were disproportionately represented in local Algerian Assemblies and with their voting power in the French National Assembly, they retained a strong political clout, virtually forcing the French government to follow their interests as far as Algerian issues were concerned. The *pieds noirs* owned a vast portion of the best land in Algeria and their individual annual income, estimated at 260,000 francs by the 1940s, was over twelve times more than that of the average indigenous Algerian. Their dominance therefore meant that any attempt to bring about equitable reforms to Algeria would be fruitless as it would conflict with their interest.

Tied to this reality was the French myth that 'Algeria is as French as Brittany,' the idea that Algeria was integrally part of France. The French colonial idea of regarding her colonies as part of France, only being located overseas (*France d'outre mer*) was thus strengthened by the power of the *pieds noirs* within the French government. The white settlers could therefore use that power to thwart any change in policy and it was difficult to find a French government willing to even consider moving against this understanding. Opposition to French colonial rule had been expressed largely by the westernized bourgeoisie in a pattern acceptable to the French rulers. The elite mostly supported the idea of integration, the French assimilation policy, which would make it easier for Algerians to acquire French citizenship and hopefully receive equal treatment. The most popular nationalist leader in the twentieth century was Hadj Messali who kept up a persistent call for an independent Algeria. He worked with the French Communist Party and opposed assimilation. He was once jailed and deported to France but continued his fight into the 1940s.

The nationalists who seemed more successful with the French government were the integrationists like Fehret Abbas, an educated Algerian who at first denied the possibility of an Algerian nation. As French hostility to meaningful change worsened, Abbas began to support a struggle for nationhood for Algeria.

Algerian nationalists in 1936 drew up a 'Charter of Demands of the Muslim Algerian People,' addressing issues of equality and respect for Muslim status. The French government decided to address some of the demands of the Charter. Reforms proposed in 1936 by the Blum government in France would have given voting rights to the middle class Algerians who would retain their Muslim status. These reforms were however prevented from being moved through the National Assembly due to opposition from the *pieds noirs* in Algeria. Failure of these reforms excited widespread nationalist sentiment going into the Second World War.

Algerians joined the Allied forces during World War II in large numbers, fighting in support of France. France's sense of gratitude was expressed by General De Gaulle and his Free French in 1942 with a proposal to re-introduce the proposed reforms of 1936. But the nationalists had moved one step higher. They had been emboldened by the nationalist reaction to the failure of the 1936 proposals and the overrunning of France by Germany during the war, making France seem to them like a weak power. The Algerian nationalists now asked for a new constitution which would address their rights. The French government only presented cosmetic reform proposals in 1944 which satisfied neither the *pieds noirs* who hotly contested the proposals, nor the nationalist elements whose impatience erupted into demonstrations. These quickly turned into riots and in May, 1945 thousands of Algerians, estimated at 50,000 by some sources, were massacred in reprisals by the French authorities. While French proposals were conceived within the framework of retaining Algeria as a French colony, the nationalists had now reached the point of demanding independence. It was certain that the impasse could only be broken by war.

Leading to the Outbreak of the Revolution

After the 1945 massacres, the French government, aided by the settlers, proceeded to tighten the instruments of suppression of opposition in Algeria. This drove the opposition underground. Elections held by the French government to the Algerian Assembly in 1946 were apparently rigged to keep out most of the militant nationalists. These latter were by then becoming disillusioned and in 1947 they formed the *Organization Speciale* (OS), a secret organization to oppose French rule 'by any means.'

The OS started recruiting a paramilitary force of young Algerian ex-soldiers, largely of peasant origin and trained in the French army. Many of these former soldiers had worked in factories in France and experienced discrimination. They were mostly unfamiliar with French glory and were more conversant with a France recently humiliated by Germany. They were ready to fight for Algerian independence from France.

French government reaction to the formation of the OS was to arrest most of the winners of the 1946 elections. By 1949 the OS had been dismantled by the police. Algeria was then in a state of undeclared war. The nationalists from the OS re-grouped and by 1953 formed the *Comité Revolutionnaire d'Unité et d'action* (CRUA), preparing for the outbreak of the revolution. The CRUA was later recognized as the *Front de Libération Nationale* (FLN). When the French government attempted to arrest some of these nationalists like Ahmed Ben Bella, they fled to Egypt where Nasser's help was paramount in supporting the revolution. From their exile, military activity was launched against the French government in Algeria in November 1, 1954.

Course of the Revolution

The soldiers of the *Armée de Libération Nationale* (ALN) numbered no more than 4,000 at the start and operations were limited to the regions of Kabylie and Oran. Though initially poorly armed with rifles and knives, by late 1955 the ranks of the ALN received significant boosting from middle class leadership in the urban areas. These urban Algerians were being victimized by the settlers and the French government, since both of the latter regarded all Algerians as potential fighters and victimized them equally.

As the war progressed, the ALN received material and financial support from other neighboring North African countries like Morocco and Tunisia, and from non-western European countries like Yugoslavia and East Germany. The population in Algeria also provided extreme support for the fighters. When Nasser seized the Suez Canal, the courage and ultimate success displayed became a big psychological boost to the Algerian fighters. This is why France was very eager for Nasser's overthrow over the Suez crisis.

Makings of the New Algerian Government

In August 1956, the FLN/ALN held its first congress in the Kabylie region of Algeria. This and subsequent meetings established the relevant structures of the movement and a strong commitment to socialist principles and agrarian reform. It also emphasized the Islamic and peasant character of the movement.

France and her Algerian settlers could not bring themselves to imagine Algeria as not being part of France. Their resolve to fight for control of Algeria was strengthened by the fact that oil had been identified in the Algerian desert and the French hoped to keep this and enrich their country. France therefore spent a lot of energy and resources to put down the revolution which only grew as many more Algerians, said to number about 130,000, joined the ranks of the freedom fighters.

French troops, numbering 56,000 at the start of the war, were said to number well over half a million before the end of the war. In order to effectively pursue the war, the French embarked on what was termed 'regrouping' of the Algerian settlements to separate the fighters from the civilian population that was giving the soldiers so much support. This regrouping amounted to herding hundreds of thousands of Algerians into virtual concentration camps. There, they could not carry on their regular economic activity and were poorly cared for so that many lives were ruined for good.

The French government also eventually succeeded in setting up electrified wire barriers between Algeria and her immediate neighbors, Morocco and Tunisia, to prevent supplies reaching the freedom fighters from these countries. The French at the same time waged a terrifying campaign of victimization, arrests and torture against the civilian population particularly with the 'battle for Algiers,' the capital. This policy of savage reprisals was to be continued by the settlers as it became clear they were losing the war. It only incited international outrage at Nazi like tactics being used by France in Algeria. None of these strategies succeeded in completely bringing down the activities of the FLN.

France Capitulates

With the war going against France and international opinion being outraged, faith in the idea of French Algeria was being shaken. In May 1958, French senior military officers in Algeria, who had acquired considerable latitude in prosecuting the war, revolted with the support of the *pieds noirs* and demanded that General de Gaulle should assume the presidency of France. They hoped by this measure to get the support of de Gaulle and his enormous reputation to finish off the war in their favor.

De Gaulle still retained the idea of a French Algeria and produced proposals for agrarian reform in the Constantine Plan, to assuage French popular opinion. This plan still created benefits for the settlers far outweighing those for the Algerian peasants and was rejected by the FLN. Neither this plan, nor a major offensive launched by the French army could destroy the revolution. In September 1958, the FLN announced the formation of a government in exile.

By the end of 1959, de Gaulle was conceding the possibility of Algerian independence. The settlers staged an unsuccessful revolt early in 1960 as they learnt that de Gaulle's government was calling for negotiations. The FLN kept up the pressure, with women playing a prominent role in planting bombs in public places like restaurants. As de Gaulle opened negotiations with the FLN in 1961, the settlers revolted again, led by senior officers of the French army. With the failure of these revolts, the settlers formed a secret army organization, the *Organisation Armée Sécrete* (OAS) and continued the most horrible terrorism against the Algerian population. As the talks moved towards a conclusion for Algerian independence, the OAS was busy killing Algerians, burning buildings and the like before they would leave Algeria.

The talks became drawn out as de Gaulle's government attempted to retain control of that part of Algeria where oil had been discovered. The FLN flatly refused and the French finally capitulated. The Evian agreement of March 1962 was put to a referendum where 99.7 percent of the Algerians voted for independence.

Morocco

The war in Algeria contributed to the advancement of the movement for independence in other North African territories. In Morocco, fitful requests by nationalist groups were not getting anywhere. One of these groups, the League for Moroccan Action, sent a delegation to Paris in 1937 and mobilized Moroccans for mass action against the French colonial rulers. As agitation broke out throughout the country, the French authorities resorted to severe repression and dissolved the League for Moroccan Action.

As events heated up in Algeria, Morocco began to stir again and its leader, Sultan Mohammed Ibn Yusuf who later became King Mohammed V, became the main focus. The Sultan became openly less patronizing to the French and the Moroccans began to follow his lead. Mass demonstrations and strikes against the French began to occur after 1947 which the French authorities and the white settlers, the *colons*, put down severely.

The sultan still continued to press for political rights supported by the Arab countries in the United Nations and the French acted to remove the sultan who had become the focus of this rising tide of anti-colonial sentiment. With the support of a small group of Arab and Berber leaders, the French in 1953 declared Yusuf as no longer fit to be sultan and he was deposed and exiled to Madagascar. A puppet was installed in his place. By the end of 1954, a 'liberation army' had been formed in some parts of Morocco which began to threaten French interests. All groups were united in their call for the return of Yusuf as sultan.

The French could not contain the increased violence and the Algerian war was getting very serious for France. The French government therefore decided to alter their policy towards Morocco. Arrangements were made for Yusuf to return and negotiations were held between the French and leading nationalists for an end to French rule in Morocco. This finally led to Morocco becoming independent in March 1956. Yusuf returned and was crowned King Mohammed V in 1957.

Tunisia

The Algerian revolution and the defeat of France in Indo-China in 1954 influenced Tunisian independence. The various Tunisian parties also encouraged by the principles of nationalism displayed at the start of the Great War, came together to form the Tunisian National Front in 1947. The Tunisian Front began to impatiently call for independence which the *colons* and the French authorities were vehemently opposed to. Negotiations between nationalist leaders and the French got nowhere and by 1952, the French took harsh repressive measures to clamp down on the nationalists. Many were arrested, some escaped to Cairo and a popular trade union leader, Farhet Hashedd was assassinated, apparently by a secret organization of the *colons*. Demonstrations broke out and acts of sabotage became widespread even among the peasant *fellaghas* in the rural areas. Settler farms were attacked and the authorities were hard put to stop the agitation.

In the face of international developments and the start of the Algerian war, the French offered internal autonomy to Tunisia. The main Neo-Destour party accepted this in 1955, anticipating this as a step in the right direction. As France faced greater problems in Algeria and Morocco, she decided to negotiate independence that would allow her to retain a good chunk of her interests in Tunisia. An agreement was therefore reached for Tunisia to become independent in March 1956.

Libya

After the scramble for Africa, Italy conquered Libya by 1916. The conquest disrupted the traditional economy leading to a steep decline in livestock. The Italians also embarked on a massive settlement of Italian peasants in Libya, a policy continued by the Italian dictator, Mussolini.

Libya was divided into three territories. One of these, Fezzan, was largely desert where isolated communities of Bedouin Arabs could be found around the oases. Tripolitania, the second division and the most populous, had a predominantly Berber population. In the third segment, Cyrenaica, the Sanusiyya Islamic order had a tradition of opposition to the Italians and its leader, Idris al-Sanusi, had been exiled by the Italians. Libyans were by and large excluded from the Italian administration of Libya.

The Second World War fell in 1939 on an impoverished and depopulated Libya. Italy was defeated in the war and this brought in British and French troops and control to Libya under the supervision of the United Nations. Cyrenaica and Tripolitania were placed under British control while Fezzan was 'given' to the French. US involvement was also present in the American establishment of an air base near Tripoli. This division and occupation of Libya was hotly contested by the Soviet Union at the United Nations.

While the western powers haggled over control of Libya, the USSR pressed for immediate independence for Libya. The British tried to strengthen her footing in Libya by supporting the return of a formerly exiled religious leader of Cyrenaica named Idris, who was then crowned as emir of Cyrenaica in 1947. Britain then had to negotiate the future of Libya with the other powers and this ended in a combination of the three territories that were then granted independence in 1951 with Idris as King Mohammed Idris I.

The western powers however retained dominance of Libya's economy. The westernized middle class in Tripolitania, which had been protesting western dominance before 1951, soon fell out with king Idris who was seen as a stooge of the western powers. All political organizations and trade unions in Libya were consequently banned in 1952. As oil was discovered in Libya soon thereafter, Libya became even more controlled by western capital and manpower. This ultimately led to reaction by the growing working class, particularly as Libya did not join in solidarity with the other Arab states in the war between the Arab states and Israel in 1967. The ensuing demonstrations and expressed dissatisfaction can be seen as the background to the military coup d'etat led by Captain Muammar Kadhaffi in 1969.

Guinea and the Rest of French West Africa

As indicated earlier, the French ruled their colonies in West (and also in Central) Africa as a large federated unit of eight colonies under a Governor-General in Dakar. After the Second World War, moves were made to give a token involvement of Africans in French politics. In 1945 the French constitution was amended to give some representation to Africans in the French Assembly. Issues African in the first Constituent Assembly after this change largely dealt with removing some odious laws affecting Africans like the abolition of the *indigénat*.

Discussions of a move towards independence were very remote. The French authorities were unequivocally opposed to independence for French colonies and the leading African politicians knew that they would be victimized if they pursued this topic. They thus satisfied themselves with addressing isolated issues of French colonial rule like the *indigénat*. These leading politicians had operated by forming parties in alliance with political parties in metropolitan France. This however did not give them much of a position in fighting for their colonies. In order to strengthen their voice these politicians formed a federal party involving all the French West African colonies. This party, called the *Rassemblement Démocratique Africain* (RDA), first met in Bamako in October, 1946. Branches of the RDA were subsequently formed in each of the territories in the federation.

The French government tried to break up the RDA, particularly in the Ivory Coast where it had appeared to become strong. This RDA branch in the Ivory Coast called the *Parti Démocratique de Côte d'Ivoire* (PDCI), was opposing privileges for French settlers in that colony and gaining widespread support thereby. The French even resorted to violent action, burning villages and arresting leaders of the PDCI. These actions frightened the RDA leaders, particularly Felix Houphouet Boigny who then threw in his loyalty to the French government.

By the 1950s, popular pressure, strikes by trade unions were erupting in French West Africa against the discriminatory policies of the French in their colonies. The French loss of the Indo-China war and the beginning of the Algerian revolution only encouraged further protest in these colonies. The French government was being forced to react on all sides and responded with a new constitution aimed at stifling the demand for total independence. This was the *Loi Cadre* of 1956 that was implemented a year later. The idea of the *Loi Cadre* was to abolish the system of keeping the French African colonies together as a federation which the French had pursued all along and which the leading African politicians were now using to strengthen their position. The *Loi Cadre* therefore set up a system of internal self-government for each territory, each with its own council of government whose president was the French governor. His vice president was an African chosen from among the majority in the council. The African politicians were expected to feel they had political power when in reality they had none.

A number of already scared politicians like Houphouet Boigny of the Ivory Coast supported the *Loi Cadre*. But younger politicians opposed it. Notable among these opponents was Ahmed Sekou Touré of the French colony of Guinea. He had been one of the founders of the RDA and defended its strength in unity to the very last. As a young man in his twenties he had been busy with trade union activity in French West Africa, initially within the framework of the French trade union system. The Guinean branch of the RDA, called the *Parti Démocratique de Guinée* (PDG) was formed by Sekou Touré. In municipal elections in Conakry, the Guinean capital late in 1956, he was elected mayor of Conakry. When the *Loi Cadre* was implemented in 1957 and elections to the councils were held, Sekou Touré's PDG won overwhelmingly in Guinea and he was elected vice president of the council, the highest position he could possible have.

Matters came to a head after de Gaulle came into office as President of France in May 1958. De Gaulle's answer to all of these developments in the French colonies was to proclaim a new constitution for France and her empire which would give full internal autonomy to each territory, removing the governor as president of the councils and creating an elected president. The colonies were however to remain ruled by France and the idea of independence was ruled out. There was to be a referendum in each of these colonies to accept or reject the new constitution and rejection meant opposing expressed French wishes and inviting the full wrath of the French government.

A flurry of political activity developed in the colonies towards this referendum that was scheduled for September 1958. Sekou Touré of Guinea and Bakary Djibo of Niger planned for a 'no' vote in their territories. The French however manipulated the elections in Niger and obtained a majority vote in support of the new constitution. No such maneuver was possible in Guinea. With his ability at grassroots organization, Sekou Touré was able to mobilize the PDG throughout the entire colony. De Gaulle visited each of the territories before the referendum to throw his weight behind his constitution. In Guinea, he was faced with organized demonstrations in favor of independence. As he left, he bade adieu to Guinea.

As the referendum gave a massive negative vote to the new constitution in Guinea, the French left immediately after with everything they could carry, and destroyed or disabled everything they could not take away including government records, medicines in hospitals, even plates in the governor's residence. Buildings and machinery were damaged. France ceased trade with and subsidies to Guinea and attempted to discourage French firms from doing business there. Guinea survived with aid from Eastern European countries and support from Kwame Nkrumah of newly independent Ghana who gave a ten million pounds sterling loan.

By the end of the 1950s decade then, Guinea, Morocco and Tunisia had achieved independence and de Gaulle was slowly conceding independence to Algeria. It was beginning to appear inevitable that France would have to grant freedom to the other French African colonies. In the scheme of things, it would be better to negotiate such a development and protect French interests, rather than enter into a costly fight. Against this background most of the French African colonies became independent in 1960. Togo, a former German colony which was a trust territory under France, had a slightly different move towards independence. The League of Nations and later the United Nations mandate under which Togo was governed tended to create some restraint on French administration here. However the French kept rigging the elections in Togo to ensure a favorable majority. By 1958, this heavy handedness was loosened and the *Comité d'Unité Togolaise* (CUT), the popular party led by Sylvanus Olympio, won elections leading to independence for Togo in 1960.

French Equatorial Africa

Independence was similarly granted in 1960 to the territories that made up French Equatorial Africa. This unit comprised the colonies of Moyen Congo based at Brazzaville, Gabon and Ubanghi-Chari. Up until the referendum of 1958 to de Gaulle's constitution, the elite in French Equatorial Africa had no thought about independence. As independence suddenly dawned on this federation, the leading African politicians there scrambled to keep the federation together. But Gabon, the richest of these colonies, feared that it would have to subsidize the other two, so Gabon objected to the continuation of the federation idea. The three territories thus became independent separately as Congo (Brazzaville), Gabon and the Central African Federation, the new name for Ubanghi-Chari.

Madagascar and Cameroon

In Madagascar, the huge island outside the western coast of southern Africa, French colonialism had created dissatisfaction among the local populace. The defeat of France in the early stages of the Second World War and subsequent British occupation of Madagascar did not help the situation in any way. At the end of the war, France, with a tarnished image in the eyes of the local elite, resumed control of Madagascar. French hostility to the idea of independence only created further nationalist hostility in Madagascar. Rebellions broke out in different parts of Madagascar in 1947 which French colonial troops suppressed only a year later. With the Algerian war and French loss in Indo-China, the nationalists were further energized. But the French manipulated local elections and this helped to keep the nationalists divided. During the referendum of 1958 on de Gaulle's constitution for a French Union, the French authorities rigged the elections to ensure a defeat for advocates of independence. Along with other French colonies in Africa, however, the French granted independence to Madagascar in June, 1960.

A similar nationalist movements in French Cameroon, emboldened by the French loss in Indo-China and the Algerian war, had resisted French efforts to manipulate it and had launched an offensive described as the 'bloody week' in 1955 which was severely put down by the French. Cameroon had been a German colony that was divided up, after Germany lost the war, between the French in the larger part, and the British in the other.

After the suppression of the 1955 disturbances, French supported parties took part in elections in 1956 and a government was set up headed by Mbida with Ahmadou Ahidjo as vice president. But the *Union des Populations du Cameroun* (UPC) which had spearheaded the 1955 disturbances and had been banned, showed it was still alive by organizing a fresh insurgency in 1957. French troops were called in and it took eleven months to put down the insurrection, capture and execute the leader of the UPC, Um Nyobe. As with the other French West African colonies, Cameroon was given independence in 1960. The UPC continued underground resistance and French troops continued to operate in Cameroon until another of the UPC leaders, Felix Moumie, was assassinated in 1960. Meanwhile, the United Nations organized a referendum in the British trust territory of the Cameroon where a northern section voted to unite with neighboring Nigeria and a southern area merged with what became the Federal Republic of Cameroon in October, 1961.

North East Africa—The Sudan

The nationalist movement in the Sudan achieved independence from Britain following the 1952 Egyptian revolution. The Sudan was technically ruled by Britain and Egypt, in reality by Britain alone, whose governor in the Sudan was all powerful. The Sudan had a dual character, the north being predominantly Arab and Islamic, while the Nilotic peoples of the south adhered to traditional religion and were increasingly influenced by western culture. The British had carried on a deliberate policy of keeping these two regions apart, stifling the spread of Islam and Arabic influence in the south where Christian missions were given every encouragement and only English was used in official matters.

The more forceful elements among the Islamic northern groups dominated, however, and their National Unionist Party, clamoring for the end of colonial rule, won elections in 1953. As the British prepared to acquiesce to their wishes, the northerners who dominated the Assembly moved to radically alter the situation in the South, making Arabic the official language and showing an open determination to control the south. Britain did not offer any opposition to this development as she was now more eager to please Egypt which was solidly behind the northern move. In December 1955, the Sudanese parliament, dominated by the north and supported by Egypt and Britain, declared for independence which was granted in January, 1956. A strong potential for conflict between the north and south still remained. In fact soldiers in the southern Equatoria Corps, the southern militia, rebelled in 1955, soon before independence and this had left much tension between the two regions.

Somalia and Ethiopia

We need to discuss the developments in the contiguous colonies of Somalia and Ethiopia together as their fortunes were closely related to each other and the unfolding of European imperialist interest in the horn of Africa. Ethiopia remained a free and independent country for the first couple of decades of the twentieth century, after defeating Italy in 1896. On the one side, Ethiopia was flanked by Somali territory where the French had a tiny colony of Afars and Issas, valued as a strategic port. Italy controlled the much greater part of Somalia, including the territory of Eritrea. Britain also had a colony in part of Somali territory.

Italy never gave up conquering Ethiopia, as Italy was piqued by her defeat at the hands of what all Europeans considered a backward African nation. Ethiopia used every strategy to keep Italy off, wooing her when necessary and joining the League of Nations, the international body set up to maintain world peace after the First World War. Ethiopia hoped that membership of the League would dissuade Italy from ambitions on Ethiopia. This proved fruitless when with a pretext and with support from Britain and France, Italy conquered and occupied Ethiopia in 1935. The invasion was very costly to Ethiopia which lost much of its infrastructure, manpower and cattle.

When the Second World War broke out and Italy joined Nazi Germany against the western allies, Britain supported a revolution in Italian occupied Ethiopia in 1942. The Ethiopian emperor, Haile Sellasie, was assisted to return to Ethiopia from exile and, with assistance from Britain, was reinstated. Since this was during the war, Britain remained the representative of the allies occupying Ethiopia until well after the end of the war. Britain also came to control Italian Somaliland as Italy lost her colonies as a result of losing the war as Germany's ally. Since Britain controlled virtually all of Somalia for a period, this helped stimulate Somali nationalism as Somalis all came together under one administration.

After Britain pulled out of most of Ethiopia in 1944, Britain decided to propose a federation between Ethiopia and Eritrea, a move endorsed by the United Nations in 1950. While some Eritrean nationalists like the Christian Tigre supported this move, others opposed it, seeking an independent Eritrea. After Eritrea joined with Ethiopia as prescribed by the UN resolution, Ethiopia proceeded to abolish the federation principle as set up in the resolution and to establish full control over Eritrea. Many opposition leaders from Eritrea went into exile and Eritrean guerilla groups started a resistance movement that was to continue for many years.

In an attempt to please Italy, the European powers pushed through in 1949 a UN decision granting Italy trusteeship of Somalia for ten years. This included British Somaliland where political developments had been stifled by the British. Under Italian rule as provided by this UN mandate Somalia gradually moved towards independence. In 1954, Britain transferred to Ethiopia the remainder of Ethiopian territory that had remained under British control. This included the Ogaden, inhabited largely by Somali peoples, and other bundles of territory called the Haud and the Reserved Area. Somali nationalists were enraged by this and mounted demonstrations in the trusteeship area under Italian rule. This activity created further political ferment which only accelerated the movement towards independence in the

Trusteeship. Political dissidents from all the Somali areas seemed to come together to call for independence, so that the former British Somaliland and Italian Somalia became independent separately in June 1960 and quickly joined together as they had already agreed. The French however continued to hold on to Afars and Issas because of its strategic port, long after the other French colonies had acceded to independence.

Questions

1. Give an account of the impact of revolutionary changes in Algeria and Egypt on other African colonies struggling for decolonization.
2. What role did Ahmed Sekou Touré play in the achievement of independence for Guinea? How different was his position from that of the other leaders in French West Africa?

Chapter XI
ഗ്രൂ
The Struggle for Independence II: Wars of Liberation

The Mau Mau Movement

It has already been mentioned that one event that influenced the achievement of independence in British African colonies, particularly those in East and Central Africa, was the Mau Mau movement in Kenya. It baffled the British, was extremely costly in men and resources and left the colonial rulers perplexed. In the end the British conceded defeat in Kenya and very quickly worked details for independence in their other African colonies.

Who organized and led the Mau Mau movement? This question has received varied answers from different interested parties. The colonialist British were firmly convinced that it was organized by the African nationalist elite in Kenya, simply because this was a way of incarcerating prominent opponents of colonial rule. While it seems clear that these elite Africans did not organize Mau Mau, it is equally evident that the Mau Mau movement, the central organizing feature of which was the oath taking, was not centrally organized by any one group, either ethnic or nationalist. It certainly dominated the Central Province of Kenya and thus was more widespread among the Kikuyu peoples. But it engulfed other non-Kikuyu regions as well. What is clear is that there was a fund of generalized discontent over colonial rule, particularly over loss of land, and this translated into a determination to oppose colonial rule. So that Mau Mau, once started, developed an engine of it's own and spread without any overarching leadership.

The primary issue of discontent was land. Much of the most fertile land had been taken over by white settlers in Kenya by the beginning of the twentieth century and Africans had been huddled into reservations. At first white farmers exploited the land they captured using cheap African labor, but allowing Africans in return to stay on the land as squatters and herd their cattle there. With the economic boom of the late 1930s onwards, the white farmers began to employ more highly mechanized agriculture. They no longer needed the African labor, now seen as a drag on their farms. The squatters were now expelled in large numbers. Some were initially settled by the colonial government but many were evicted for disobeying agricultural instructions.

These evictions created widespread discontent and brought back awareness of the loss of the land half a century earlier. While they stayed on the white owned land as squatters, the pain of loss had been mitigated. Now that they were evicted with no viable alternative, this was even more painful. Moreover, in the relatively fertile Kikuyu reserves, population growth meant competition for the land which had become inadequate for the people, while whites had abundant and fertile land. Colonial government commissions to look into the land problem never satisfied the African population while this same government was introducing, in the name of agricultural improvement, measures like rinderpest control and terracing. These moves stifled the agricultural practices of the Africans, in their own perception, and sometimes meant that the colonial authorities had to kill some of the cattle of the Africans.

It is these generalized economic grievances that led to the start of oath taking as a means of committing people to participate in actions that would help bring down the colonial government. It seems from available evidence that it was mostly younger militants mainly from Nairobi, who associated with trade union activities that had been planning armed insurrection against the colonial government. The oath became an important way of securing loyalty and participation and quickly spread after the Second World War.

The importance of the oath in most African cultures needs to be explained. An oath was a sacred and binding undertaking that no one thought of violating. Often administered in traditional ritual with secret herbal concoctions, the oath was believed powerful enough to destroy anyone who took it and violated the dictates that went with it. The oath was therefore an extremely powerful instrument in securing compliance in community wide action. The leaders of the movement employed this to effect and mounted oath-taking campaigns in many communities.

The oath campaign had started a few years before the colonial government took notice of it. In 1951 there was widespread rioting against rinderpest regulations and compulsory terracing. Following the rioting white settler farms were set on fire, their cattle maimed and a prominent Kikuyu loyal to the colonial government was killed by gunmen in broad daylight. It was then that the colonial rulers took notice of Mau Mau and started taking action against the movement. It is believed that Mau Mau means 'the greedy eaters,' a term applied to the movement by its enemies.

One of the moves of the colonialists in response to Mau Mau was to blame the movement on the African bourgeoisie and take consequent action against that group. The main group of the African middle class here was the Kenya African Union (KAU), founded in 1944 as a moderate organization to support African political rights. In 1947 Jomo Kenyatta returned to Kenya from exile in Britain to lead the KAU in protesting colonial rule. The British quickly arrested and detained Kenyatta and other KAU leaders as instigators of Mau Mau. They were given a rough and ready trial and sent to jail. Apart from the fact that these leaders sympathized with Mau Mau, there was hardly any evidence that the movement was led by Kenyatta and the others arrested.

By 1952, Mau Mau activity had come to be regarded as very threatening to the white settlers and the government declared a state of emergency thereby conferring on itself special powers to deal with the situation. This only appeared to strengthen the Mau Mau movement which moved against all Kikuyu suspected of aiding the colonialists. Thousands lost their lives in consequence. But these were mostly Africans as relatively few Europeans were killed in the time of the entire movement. The colonial government brought in British troops and developed a policy of 'villagization,' removing people from their villages into virtual concentration camps when it was realized that Mau Mau had strong support from the population. Believing Mau Mau to be a military threat, the government used tanks, bombs and armored vehicles to destroy the highland camps of the movement. But oath making and violence only increased and in spite of all these efforts and expenditure, Mau Mau remained strong.

The Mau Mau cost the British about fifty million pounds sterling, a colossal sum by the standards of the time. It also meant that a large section of the British army was quartered in Kenya. A new colonial secretary in Britain in 1959 finally came to his senses, realizing the futility of such enormous expenditure to protect the British settlers in Kenya. The state of emergency was ended in 1960 and Kenyatta released from prison in 1961.

Protracted negotiations, including constitutional conferences continued for another couple of years as the settlers, supported by British machinations, tried to find more pliable alternative African leadership to the immensely popular Kenyatta. In the end however, Kenyatta's Kenya African National Union (KANU) scored an overwhelming victory in elections held in May 1963 and Kenya became independent that same year with Kenyatta as Prime Minister and head of government.

The Gold Coast and the Rest of West Africa

Parallel to the Mau Mau movement was the acceleration of the nationalist movement in the Gold Coast Colony. Kwame Nkrumah was invited home to the Gold Coast by J.B. Danquah to help revitalize the United Gold Coast Convention (UGCC). Bringing back home his organizational and militant experience particularly with the Pan-African Congress of 1945, Nkrumah quickly fell out with the more conservative UGCC leadership after he and other UGCC leaders were blamed for having instigated anti-colonial civil disturbances and detained in 1948. Nkrumah soon formed his own Convention Peoples Party (CPP) three months later. He then established *The Accra Evening News* as an organ to promote his party. He published in the same year a pamphlet on Positive Action which was to be his watchword.

Nkrumah's Positive Action campaign involved a cry for 'self government now.' This was a radical move as was the CPP he had founded. Nkrumah mobilized the youth of Accra and leading towns, including the unemployed who had little to lose. He toured different regions of the Gold Coast and also mobilized the support of trade unions. Much of this activity which Nkrumah had started with the UGCC he now carried into the CPP which became a mass party.

In the face of threats of violence, the British were revising the constitution for the Gold Coast, making minor cosmetic changes. Nkrumah launched a 'Positive Action' campaign which led to mass action especially by trade unions. He was arrested again by the British, convicted and jailed for his part in the anti-colonial disturbances. From jail Nkrumah directed the CPP to victory in the elections called by the British in 1951. The British governor was then forced to release him and appoint him leader of government business in parliament. Pressure from Nkrumah and the CPP led to a new constitution in 1954 that provided for an elected majority in parliament on the basis of which the Gold Coast was granted independence as Ghana in 1957.

By the time of Ghana's independence, the British had clearly accepted the principle of independence for the other territories in West Africa and would rather grant these peacefully than incur costly struggles like Mau Mau. Internal interests were thus accommodated and Nigeria became independent in 1960, Sierra Leone in 1961 and the tiny colony of the Gambia in 1965.

The Portuguese Colonies

Portuguese rule extended over the large colonies of Mozambique and Angola and the tiny West African territory of Guinea-Cape Verde and the islands of Sao Tome and Principe. As mentioned before Portugal had an excessive dependence on her African colonies and had no intention to relinquish control even in the face of the rapid move towards independence all around her African colonies by the beginning 1960s. Portugal had encouraged massive migration from Portugal to Angola and Mozambique so that the white settler population in Angola for example had increased almost four times in the twenty years between 1950 and 1970.

Unrest among the African population, buoyed by a movement for liberation in other African colonies, met with harsh repression by the Portuguese authorities. In 1961 in Mozambique, at a meeting called by Portuguese authorities to listen to local grievances at the Mueda Administrative District, troops opened fire killing hundreds of protestors. In that same year, when agrarian unrest provoked violence, the Portuguese air force bombed a number of villages. This was followed by a rampage of white settlers, killing hundreds of blacks and spreading violence through much of Angola.

A dock workers' strike in Guinea-Bissau in 1959 met with similar repression from the Portuguese. This gave a booster to a young political party that had been formed in 1956 called the *Partido Africano da Independencia da Guiné e Cabo Verde* (PAIGC). This party was led by Amilcar Cabral, one of the very few Africans from Guinea-Bissau who had acquired some western education. As the party and its program for unconditional independence became known, the Portuguese authorities swooped down on it, only to generalize an armed struggle in the countryside which had already been conditioned for this development by Cabral's activities. Cabral was unfortunately assassinated in January 1974, soon before the end of the struggle.

In Mozambique, the liberation movement coalesced in neighboring Tanzania with the encouragement of that country's new leader, Julius Nyerere. A couple of earlier organizations of Mozambique exiles met in Tanzania in 1962 and formed the *Frente de Libertação de Mocambique* (FRELIMO), or the Front for the Liberation of Mozambique. It was Frelimo with its chosen leader, Eduardo Mondlane, which planned a war of liberation starting in 1963. As the war began to score successes in the countryside, the Portuguese colonialists moved to infiltrate the movement. They teamed up with dissidents and this ended with the assassination of Mondlane by a parcel bomb in Tanzania in 1969. Mondlane was replaced by Samora Machel who continued the war.

The Angolan liberation movement, the *Movimento Popular de Libertação de Angola* (MPLA) had been formed since 1955 and quickly became the guiding hand behind the struggle to remove Portuguese rule from Angola. By 1961, the MPLA had set up a base not too distant from Luanda, the capital, and its operations became obvious. There were other dissident political units in Angola with the same objective, particularly the *Uniao Nacional para a Independencia total de Angola* (UNITA) and the *Frente nacional de Libertaçao de Angola* (FNLA).

The liberation war particularly in Angola became entangled with the cold war. The declared Marxist leanings of the MPLA became an important reason for the US to provide outright support for Portugal against the freedom fighters, since the US was bent on opposing any communist foothold in this region. This strengthened the Portuguese to counter the activities of these liberation movements more effectively and to keep them from coming together. The Portuguese also moved much of the population into concentration camps that they called "protected villages," to keep them away from the liberation fighters and thus prevent the latter from getting any assistance from the local population.

Cold war interests and US policy of supporting white minority regimes placed the United States and apartheid South Africa on the same side against the liberation struggle in the Portuguese colonies. South Africa had added reason to support the Portuguese against the guerilla fighters. The United Nations Trust territory of South West Africa, which had common borders with Angola and South Africa, had been entrusted to South Africa's supervision. South Africa's determination to integrally absorb South West Africa had put South Africa at odds with the United Nations. The Nationalist

Movement in South West Africa that was continuously hounded by the South African authorities, had come together into a single organization called the South West African Peoples Organization (SWAPO). This movement had also launched a war of liberation against South Africa by 1969.

It was important to South Africa that Portugal remained in control of Angola so that SWAPO fighters would find it difficult to use Angola as a base for launching attacks into South West Africa. Portugal's domination of both Angola and Mozambique also worked in the interest of South Africa since a friendly Portugal would not allow the African National Congress (ANC) to use these neighboring territories as bases in its fight against the racist South African regime. A coalition of international and South African interests was therefore working in favor of continued colonial domination and against the interests of the nationalist soldiers in Southern Africa.

The massive support that Portugal received from the United States and other western governments did not suffice to stymie the militant nationalist movements. In the end, it was Portugal's war fatigue that decided the issue. By the early 1970s, Portugal was spending about half of its annual resources on these colonial wars. Conscription in Portugal was creating much hostility among the population. With mounting hostility against the colonial wars even in the army, President Caetano who had succeeded the dictator, Salazar, was removed from office in a military coup d'etat in April 1974. A ruling junta was set up headed by General Spinola, known to be opposed to the colonial war. This new Portuguese government hastily signed the Lusaka Agreement with the nationalist fighters by September and Angola and Mozambique became independent in 1975. Portugal reached similar agreements with Guinea Bissau which became independent in September 1974. It was also in 1975, following similar circumstances, that Portugal granted independence to the island territories of Sao Tome and Principe.

South West Africa (Namibia)

Independence for Angola meant greater Angolan support for SWAPO. To counter this, the South African government often invaded Angolan territory, ostensibly to pursue SWAPO guerillas. In the process, the South African forces were aiding the UNITA movement which had started a civil war against the MPLA government in newly independent Angola. The MPLA's reliance on communist help, particularly Cuban troops, simply solidified US and South African support behind the UNITA rebels. UNITA was based in southern Angola and in 1982 South African forces occupied a large area of Southern Angola for an extended period. The power of the South African army with US support was used to wring an agreement from Angola to stop supporting SWAPO.

In the end, major changes in the 1980s turned the tables in favor of SWAPO. The break up of the Soviet Union signaled the end of the cold war making it unnecessary for the US to provide anti-communist support. The racist regime in South Africa also collapsed, removing South African hostility to South West Africa. An agreement was arrived at with United Nations support in December, 1988. Elections followed in November 1989 and SWAPO won with a large majority. Independence thus came to South West Africa with the new name of Namibia in March, 1990.

The High Commission Territories

The three southern African colonies of Basutoland, Bechuanaland and Swaziland had been administered by the British through High Commissioners, British officials or agents who were involved with the South African government. While these were British colonies, they were virtually controlled by South Africa and at certain points the British were not opposed to a South African administration over these colonies.

Independence for the territories of Basutoland, Bechuanaland and Swaziland came after Britain had become committed to the principle of independence for her colonies. An important concern for the Africans in these territories that were either surrounded by or lengthily bordered South Africa was the interest the white minority regimes in South Africa had in controlling these territories. The British could not arrive at any agreement with apartheid South Africa for the administration of these colonies. This factor, plus agitation by African groups in the colonies, ensured that these three remained separate entities. British maneuvers finally ended with new constitutions for these colonies that became independent in succession. Basotuland became Lesotho in October 1966; Bechuanaland assumed the new name of Botswana in September 1966 and Swaziland assumed independent status with the same name in 1969.

White Settler Minorities
in the Central African Federation

Settler minorities in Nyasaland, Northern and Southern Rhodesia helped to create a more problematic transition in Central Africa, even though the British had become committed to the granting of independence. At issue was the imposition in 1953 of a Central African Federation (CAF) that included Northern and Southern Rhodesia and Nyasaland. The white minority of Southern Rhodesia had acquired internal self-government from the British since 1923. The Southern Rhodesian whites wished to control the other two territories through the political ploy of a federation, and needed British government support to achieve this. In 1951, a new Conservative government in Britain looked favorably on the idea and imposed this Federation in 1953, in spite of protests led by the African elite in Northern Rhodesia and Nyasaland. Riots broke out in Nyasaland in consequence.

Intended to entrench white control, the CAF also helped to stimulate African nationalism in these colonies and make it more vocal. The government of the CAF, after inauguration, proceeded to strengthen white control while creating an appearance of making concessions to African interests. White immigration was encouraged and laws were passed to give only whites the vote. With Mau Mau going against the British government and white settlers in Kenya, the British began to rethink its support for the CAF and white minority rule in these other three colonies.

Meanwhile the nationalist movements in these colonies were energized. In Nyasaland, with much fewer white settlers, the Nyasaland African Congress was revived with younger, more radical leaders. It quickly solidified around Dr. H. Kamuzu Banda who returned from Britain to Nyasaland in 1958 to be regarded as the undisputed leader of the nationalist movement. In Northern Rhodesia, too, Kenneth Kaunda emerged as leader of protest by the same time, forming the Zambian African National Congress to fight for full independence.

With nationalist movements becoming strong also in Southern Rhodesia, the British moved to ban these movements and arrest their leaders. Commissions set up to investigate and strengthen the federation only discovered that African opinion was united against it. As tension mounted, the British gave in and agreed to give independence with majority rule to Nyasaland. This signaled the breakup of the CAF in 1963 and Nyasaland became independent with the new name of Malawi in 1964 under Banda as president. Northern Rhodesia followed suit the same year under Kenneth Kaunda and assumed the new name of Zambia.

Southern Rhodesia (Zimbabwe)

With the breakup of the CAF, the white settlers of Southern Rhodesia became even more determined to retain control of the government and use their military to enforce the compliance of the Africans there. Since Southern Rhodesia was self-governing, the British government was not inclined to forcefully intervene. The most extremist elements in the white minority government, represented in the Rhodesian Front Party, in fact gained ascendancy in elections in 1962 and enacted laws to ban or severely restrict African political activity. Britain was however inclined to insist on black majority rule as was unfolding in the neighboring British colonies. Unwilling to accept this, the Rhodesian Front government under Ian Smith proceeded to unilaterally declare independence off Britain in 1965. The United Nations, on Britain's urgings, imposed economic sanctions on Rhodesia, as it came to be called. Support from the Portuguese in neighboring Angola and Mozambique, and the apartheid government of neighboring South Africa ensured that the sanctions did not work. In fact Zambia, a land locked country suffered more from the sanctions since it had received much of her supplies through Rhodesia.

Britain had earlier declared it would not use force against the Rhodesian Front government. As it began to appear that there would be no end to the white minority government in Rhodesia, the African parties in Rhodesia, the Zimbabwe African National Union (ZANU) and the Zimbabwe African Peoples Union (ZAPU) launched an armed struggle against the white minority government by 1965.

As the civil war gathered momentum, the Smith regime in Rhodesia engaged in a series of deliberations with Britain. But Britain was unwilling to use force against the racist Rhodesian regime. This regime had the tacit support of the United States government whose policy was to support white minority governments. The Rhodesian Front government of Ian Smith also had support and assistance from the Portuguese rulers of neighboring Angola and Mozambique, and from apartheid South Africa. The Zimbabwe liberation armies however gradually gained the confidence of the rural population in Rhodesia, as well as in areas in Mozambique already controlled by other liberation fighters in that colony who were fighting against the Portuguese government. The rebel armies had bases in Zambia and Mozambique that were constantly attacked by the Rhodesian army.

When Portuguese rule in southern Africa fell and Mozambique and Angola became independent in 1975, the Smith regime lost valuable buffers on its flanks. It then became more prone to compromise in talks with the British and to accommodate African interests. African leaders who had been detained were released. Two of these leaders, Joshua Nkomo of the Zimbabwe African People's Union (ZAPU) and Robert Mugabe, of the

Zimbabwe African National Union (ZANU), then formed the Patriotic Front (PF) which intensified the armed struggle. An internal settlement supported by Britain was worked out in 1978. By this agreement Bishop Abel Muzorewa, a moderate identified by the Smith regime, and who lead a black coalition called the United African National Congress (UANC) would become head of a new government sharing power with the white minority. This agreement was implemented but was boycotted by the PF and the short-lived Muzorewa government ended up joining Ian Smith in a war against the PF.

By the late 1970s the tide was clearly against the white minority in Rhodesia, with South Africa becoming lukewarm in its support. Another conference in Britain in 1979 resolved the issue bringing majority rule. Elections in 1980 were won by the ZANU branch of the PF with Robert Mugabe becoming the head of government. Rhodesia became independent as Zimbabwe in April, 1980

Tanganyika and Zanzibar

Political activity leading to independence in Tanganyika was given a huge fillip by the success of the Mau Mau rebellion in Kenya which impacted on the willingness of the British to decolonize. Welfare associations, notably the Tanganyika African Association (TAA) were making little headway before then, as the British too reacted by transferring some of its more vocal leaders from the capital, Dar Es Salaam in order to weaken the movement. When Julius Nyerere arrived from studies in Britain in 1952, he provided the necessary glue to galvanize the TAA into a popular political party called the Tanganyika African National Union (TANU). Nyerere also exploited Tanganyika's position as a United Nations Trust Territory, capitalizing on international support for decolonization. By 1960, the British allowed the first freely contested elections to the Tanganyikan Legislative Council. TANU won almost all the seats. Nyerere became leader of government with Tanganyika gaining independence in December, 1961.

The adjacent Zanzibar Island had been an Arab dominated center of East African trade since the nineteenth century. It became a British colony during the scramble for Africa and was granted independence by Britain in December 1963. The Arab minority of Zanzibar had continued to dominate the African population and fought to gain independence off Britain before any British program for majority rule would be brought in. The elections before independence were manipulated to give an Arab majority and with independence, Arabs replaced the British in all senior positions. One month later an African originally from Uganda named John Okello mobilized a small loyalist force which staged a bloody revolution in Zanzibar. The leaders of the successful revolution then negotiated amalgamation with Tanganyika and the two become the United Republic of Tanzania in April 1964.

Uganda

British colonial rule in Uganda had concentrated on the kingdom of Buganda, the largest pre-colonial unit in what came to be the colony of Uganda. The other smaller units were disgruntled at this but there was also general dissatisfaction against Asian dominance in the economy and the British did not seem concerned about this matter. Unrest with an economic background later crystallized into support for Milton Obote's Uganda National Congress (UNC) which was agitating for responsible government. When the British governor exiled the *Kabaka* (king) of Buganda in 1955, nationalist sentiment crystallized into a cry for a restoration of Kabaka Mutesa II.

The UNC disintegrated after a short while, and was replaced by a new party, the Uganda People's Congress (UPC) which won pre-independence elections in 1962. A coalition of different interests was headed by the UPC leader, Milton Obote, who became head of an independent Uganda later in 1962.

Inevitable Independence in Central Africa—The Congo

By the end of the decade of the 1950s, virtually all colonial powers were under pressure, both external from the United Nations, and internal from political groups to grant independence to their colonies. The rapid move towards independence in the far more numerous British and French colonies by that time also expedited the issue. This was the background to the situation in the Belgian Congo where the Belgians had earlier taken the view of 'no elites, no trouble.' Thus those who became the leaders of the Congo had received very little western education to enable them to operate in the western based system set up by colonial rule. The first black man allowed to enter a Belgian university did so in 1952. Cultural organizations like the *Association des Bakongo* (ABAKO) were led by a very docile westernized elite. Ostensibly triggered by developments in neighboring French Congo, the Belgian rulers allowed municipal elections in December 1957, the first of which took place in Leopoldville (later called Kinshasa) and was won by Joseph Kasavabu, leader of ABAKO. Political activity was thus started up and Patrice Lumumba formed the *Mouvement National Congolais* in October 1958. These local elections in the next few months ignited the smoldering embers of economic and social discontent and exploded into rioting in Leopoldville in January 1959.

Fearing a situation similar to the Algerian war, the Belgian government suddenly capitulated and a week after the rioting announced its intention of granting independence to the Congo. A flood of uncoordinated nationalist political activity quickly developed in response to this. A round table conference called in Brussels in January 1960 set the date for independence as June 30, 1960. The sharply divided elite formed movements to control regional interests even as the Belgians hurriedly granted independence. Three governments emerged. There was a central government with Kasavubu as president and Lumumba as prime minister or leader of government business. In existence also was a regional secessionist government led by Moise Tshombe in control of the mineral wealthy Katanga province which Belgian and European settler interest came to support. Lumumba's government soon lost control of the situation and he was dismissed by President Kasavabu. A third government was simultaneously set up in the town of Stanleyville by Antoine Gizenga who had been Lumumba's deputy. As chaos and uncertainty reigned, the army under Joseph Mobutu seized control at the capital and Lumumba was arrested. Lumumba was later assassinated in prison and it was believed that this was done with the collusion of the western powers. Lumumba's Marxist leanings obviously made him a threat in the heat of the cold war. Mobutu finally asserted his control over all the other factions by 1965 and became the undisputed head of state.

Rwanda, Burundi and Spanish Equatorial Africa

Rwanda and Burundi, two tiny states in central Africa sharing common borders with the Democratic Republic of the Congo, progressed rapidly towards independence following the sudden Belgian decision to pull out of the Congo. Both colonies had become Trust territories ruled by Belgium when the former colonial power, Germany, lost her colonies following her defeat in the First World War. There are two major ethnic groups in the two states, both speaking the same language. These are the minority Tutsi, a cattle-keeping people, and the majority Hutu. Belgium, like Germany before her, had been promoting the Tutsi minority and stifled any social and economic advancement among the Hutu majority which was ruthlessly exploited.

Quite suddenly in 1959, Belgium's plan to move these colonies rapidly towards independence indicated support for a Hutu majority rule. Elections of 1960 were consequently won by a Hutu party and the Hutu took this cue from the Belgians to fall on the Tutsi. Many Tutsi were killed or fled to neighboring countries. The United Nations stepped in and conducted pre-independence elections in 1961 which were won by Hutu parties. Rwanda's administration was separated from that of Burundi and both became independent in 1962. Dangerous tension between Hutu and Tutsi was thus left behind.

In Equatorial Guinea, Spain had ignored any protest until the 1950s, but came under pressure at the United Nations and from Afro-Asian countries after 1955 when Spain joined that international body. Spanish repression led to the assassination of Acacio Mane in 1958 and Enrique Nvo in 1959, two leading local politicians in Equatorial Guinea. Others fled to neighboring Cameroons and Gabon and continued political protest from there. After most African countries became independent and began supporting the Equatorial Guinea liberation movement in exile, Spain began to give in. Political parties were recognized in 1963 and internal self rule in 1964. Independence was finally granted in October 1968.

Questions

1. How significant was the Mau Mau movement in the decolonization process in Africa?
2. Discuss the role of white settler interest in the drive towards independence in Central Africa.

Chapter XII

ဧသ

The Political Economy of Decline in Post-Colonial Africa

The rest of the twentieth century, since the 1960s, has witnessed a continuing deterioration in African economies, in the quality of life of their peoples and in attendant political instability in most African states. If one is to believe the western media and apologists, including major segments of the western oriented African elite, this is entirely the fault of inept African leaders, clamoring to suppress their peoples and hold on to power while enriching themselves out of public funds.

Part of this argument holds true in most instances. It is difficult to see however what striking progress the economies have made in the few African countries like Botswana, Senegal, Kenya, where the leaders have held the faith, maintained western style democracy and where corruption is similar to that in developed countries. At least part of the explanation for this decline must then rest elsewhere, at the doorstep of the former colonial powers and their western allies, still bent on exploiting African countries while giving the distinct impression of doing good and helping Africans who always make the wrong policy decisions or follow the wrong path. This is the kind of message put forward in the global media controlled by these same western nations. Let us then attempt to examine the factors that have contributed to the contemporary situation in Africa.

The Euphoria of Independence

At independence, Africans were filled with high expectations. I remember as a senior high school student in Sierra Leone at midnight on April 26, 1961 when the British flag was being lowered at an impressive public ceremony and the Sierra Leone flag was hoisted, ushering the dawn of independence. I developed goose bumps as the national song was played by the military, accompanying the event. I saw barely literate old women in the streets surrounding the public arena shouting 'thank God almighty, we are free!'

This euphoria was shared by governments that believed in the new opportunities for improving the lives of the populace with more widespread western education, more hospitals, good roads and higher salaries. These values were unquestionably assumed by all Africans to accompany this freedom.

In consequence, African governments in the first years of independence attempted to give expressions to these aspirations, to expand basic infrastructure and social services. Members of the new parliaments had competing interests to satisfy to ensure that their constituencies had water supply, electricity, schools and hospitals. All of this expansion came at a price, for colonial rule did not leave behind booming economies, nor was foreign aid very lavish. None of these economies was supported by industry or expanding agriculture, so that satisfying these needs soon became a serious economic burden to the African countries.

Nature of African Economies

The economies of these African countries were largely carried over from the late colonial period. What was carried over involved an emphasis on production of commodities as raw materials for export. These raw materials included minerals in some instances, but overwhelmingly they were agricultural products—coffee, cocoa, ginger, rubber—unprocessed for export. Because of the emphasis of the colonial governments on these cash crops, as they were called, production had shifted gradually away from food crop production so that not too long after independence African countries had become net importers of food to feed their own populations. In fact importing basic foodstuff had come to be encouraged by some post-colonial governments as a way of getting kickbacks, to the continued detriment of food production.

The sale of these cash crops was part of international commerce controlled by the developed countries. One prominent feature of this commerce was the continuing decline in the terms of trade for the developing, mostly African countries. Prices of these cash crops were fixed by the developed countries and these prices, which had been improving in the late colonial period, went into decline after independence, hitting the economies of certain countries very badly. The price of copper, for example, on which the Democratic Republic of the Congo (then called Zaire) depended, declined very sharply in the mid 1970s. Fluctuating price of cocoa similarly did havoc to the economies of Ghana, heavily dependent on this crop. From 1970-1984, Africa's world market share of coffee, cocoa and cotton progressively fell by 13, 33, and 29 per cent.

While the cost of these cash crop exports from African countries continued to decline, the cost of manufactured goods imported by the African countries continued to rise. The prices of both cash crops and manufactured goods were fixed by the same developed countries. African countries therefore received less money for what they sold and had to find more cash to pay for the manufactured goods they bought.

African governments attempted to control the local sale of these cash crops and minerals as the colonial governments had done, to provide incomes for government business. This meant paying prices to the actual producers lower than the world market prices to the dissatisfaction of farmers who sometimes got wise enough to boycott the government buying systems. Often, incomes coming to the farmers from the sale of these commodities were manipulated by governments, providing avenues for excessive corruption by politicians and bureaucrats.

As far as mining of minerals was concerned, many of the mining concessions had been doled out to western consortiums on extremely liberal terms soon before independence. The argument at that time would have been that the profits ultimately went to the same countries of the colonial rulers. After independence, some African governments made strenuous attempts to re-negotiate these liberal contracts as well as, where necessary, to develop new contracts on new minerals. Multi National Corporations (MNCs) and similar concerns, intent on keeping their liberal contracts or on making new agreements favorable to themselves, readily bribed these new and inexperienced African politicians and bureaucrats.

This pattern of bribery which started after independence has continued apace into contracts to build roads, to start new factories, etc. Information about such bribery surface every now and again, but are scanty, since these arrangements were done off the record and neither party was keen on divulging such information. If one wonders at the rate at which corruption permeated the African political scene, then one has to consider the role of these agents of the developed world in this outcome. For African politicians and bureaucrats, derived from the new elite whose values we discussed earlier, did not distinguish much between western government or private sector representatives who came to Africa, well dressed in business suits. To the African leaders, these representatives of the western world came from the same culture that Africans believed to be the paragon of honesty and integrity. If these Western interests could readily bribe top politicians and bureaucrats, then these African leaders would want to believe that this was a normal element of government in the developed world. It snowballed from there.

Mining therefore provided little by way of revenue to many African governments. MNCs always pointed to their provision of jobs in the local African economies from the mining. But the profits were supposed to be shared equally as the African countries provided the minerals and the MNCs brought the expertise to extract them. This parity of benefits never materialized as, apart from bribery, these western business interests controlled the marketing of the minerals and could use transfer pricing and other techniques to ensure that the African countries benefited little from their minerals.

Another factor which also militated against African countries getting the best terms from these contracts was a lack of adequate qualified technical expertise to negotiate and monitor fulfillment with the savvy agents of MNCs. There were very few qualified Africans in many areas at independence. While African governments pushed to remedy this deficiency, they still remained at the mercy of the developed world agents. The Africans who signed these contracts on behalf of their governments therefore were not very familiar with the nature or language of the contracts. Most of these contracts were 'negotiated' in the western capitals where the relatively poor and easily tempted African negotiators were feasted and entertained lavishly, diverting their attention away from the details of the contracts. When all of these factors are coupled with bribery on the part of the MNCs, it can be seen how African countries benefited least form their natural resources.

The lack of adequate technical expertise in these African countries, coupled with the attitude of the elite African rulers that representatives of western economies knew better and would act in the best interest of the Africans, brought many western 'experts' to help run African economies.

Even the best intentioned among these were often unfamiliar with the local situation and therefore with the best remedies. Many of these 'experts' never stayed long enough to fully get to grips with the problems. In many instances also, hegemonic arrogance on the part of these western 'experts' kept them from accepting their own shortcomings and learning from the Africans on the spot. The net result was often at best a sense of direction provided by these 'experts' at variance with the needs of these African countries, at worst a deliberate distortion of the situation so as to benefit the developed countries at the expense of the African Peoples.

Oil Price Hikes

An additional problem most African countries faced was the cost of energy. Energy in the 'modern' sector of the African economies was mostly dependent on oil that most African countries, except a few like Gabon, Angola, Nigeria and the North African countries, did not possess. In the beginning 1970s, oil producing countries in the developing world, most of them Arab, decided to come together in an organization that would secure their interests in the pricing of the oil they produced. The result was the Organization of Petroleum Exporting Countries (OPEC) that included some African countries like Algeria, Libya and Nigeria. OPEC decided to limit production and sale of crude oil so as to raise the price of this commodity to the benefit of its members. Thus began a series of sharp rises in the price of crude oil, three of these oil price shocks occurring in the 1970s.

African countries that were not oil producing were hard hit by this development. The cost to Tanzania of the oil price hike in the 1970s for example meant virtually a nine-fold increase in what she had to pay for oil imports by 1981. Tanzania's oil imports in 1972 amounted to 269 million shillings, its local currency. In 1977, after reducing her oil imports to eighty percent of the 1972 levels, Tanzania had to pay 835 million shillings for crude oil. Further reductions in oil import were made in 1981 to seventy percent of 1972 levels. Still Tanzania had to pay 2050 million shillings for crude oil imports.

The impact of the oil price hikes was similar in most African countries. The developed countries, affected by the increase in crude oil prices, simply increased the cost of manufactured goods so that some of them ended with a net profit from this development. Again, this meant higher import bills for manufactured goods for the poor African countries.

Drought

We must add to this picture an unending cycle of drought in the sahel, that region running along the southern Sahara in northern Africa. The drought phenomenon also extended along the rift valley, hitting squarely countries in eastern and southern Africa. There was an extended drought in the sahel region from 1968 to 1974, hitting as well areas of East Africa from 1974-1976. Periods of drought between 1983 and 1985 and into the rest of the 1980s hit over 39 countries in Africa, affecting over 35 million people. Countries like Mali, Burkina Faso, Ethiopia, Sudan, Niger, Tanzania, Somalia, Senegal, Mozambique are often hardest hit. In Ethiopia alone, about one million people reportedly died from the drought, which worsened an already poor food and agricultural situation. Southern Africa was hit by a severe drought in 1993 and one was reported in Kenya by 2000.

The nature of this drought may not readily be comprehended by people in western countries, unfamiliar with this kind of situation. It means no water from rainfall for an extended period, sometimes running into a couple of years. With water storage capacity being low in these countries, water soon runs out and crops do not grow and domestic animals die. Famine results and large sections of the population are immobilized or die due to malnutrition, lack of resistance to consequent disease and hunger. Coping with this type of situation diverts a considerable portion of the already meager resources of these African countries to drought relief.

Developed countries often attributed the drought to the expansion of the Sahara desert which in turn was blamed on deforestation by unconscionable African farmers, indiscriminately cutting down trees for farms and firewood. As usual, Africans are held responsible for whatever calamities befall them. More recent research has however suggested that the expansion of the Sahara would be due to major shifts in the global climate scene rather than to profligate African farmers.

The Political Complex

Many of the problems affecting the economies mentioned above are exacerbated by the political situation in the African countries. African countries inherited from colonial rule political systems with which the vast majority of the population was completely unfamiliar. Colonial rule had involved an extremely authoritarian political rule that brooked no opposition. Dissenting opinions were tolerated only if they did not threaten the body politic. There were no representative political institutions that existed only in the white settler colonies for white settlers alone. Two generations of Africans therefore grew up in colonial systems that gave them the impression that politics meant an intolerant control of power.

Just before the end of the colonial period, representative institutions were suddenly introduced to these colonies in very modified forms. These were not institutions that operated in the colonies exactly as they did in France or Britain, the ruling colonial countries. Of course Portugal never followed this pattern and in the Belgian Congo, it was almost exactly a year before independence when the new politics started. Control of this new political system was literally handed to the elite, that group of western indoctrinated Africans who had been taught to believe they were superior to the rest of the population for having acquired western values and education, often only a limited aspect of these. The vast majority of the population had absolutely no way of knowing how western style representative political institutions worked, the role of the press or civil society, and the element of political power being vested in the people who choose representatives to look after the people's interests. They were never educated to learn that representatives could be removed through voting where a free and informed system would educate them about what these representatives had been up to. In short, there was no political education for the vast majority of the African peoples emerging from colonial rule.

The new western oriented political systems therefore placed a small group of hungry, often poor Africans who had some western training in charge of the destiny of a population ignorant of how to be watchdogs of these new leaders. These latter themselves faced the daunting task of ruling new nations for which they had no experience but had to contend with political and economic forces from the developed world that were certainly not working in their interests. With a little taste of political power, these new presidents sought to retain themselves in office. All they needed to do was to manipulate weak constitutions not vested in the power of the people. Some of the tools they could readily use to achieve this were of course state resources they now controlled and elements like ethnicity.

Ethnicity and Corruption in Politics

The reality of a multiplicity of ethnic groups existed in these states with inherited political boundaries. By and large, different ethnic groups had always co-existed side by side. The desire to exclusively control the new politics however meant that political leaders had to appeal to issues other than democratic ones to sway a majority. To a populace that knew little better about the new politics, 'vote for me because we belong to the same ethnic group' sounded as good an argument as any for political support. Political leaders therefore picked on ethnicity as freely as possible, particularly when their positions were threatened, which happened very frequently.

Weak governmental systems, weak constitutions and a largely uninformed populace were a perfect prescription for authoritarian rulers. These new rulers quickly began to develop their own versions of political systems suitable to their exercise of exclusive power. This meant that opposition and dissent were threats to their positions and these were destroyed with varying degrees of brute force.

Political leaders strengthened their positions by appropriating state resources for the use of their party. The state and the ruling party became identified as one and the same unit. The rulers also used this control of power to enrich themselves. Since fragile constitutions were altered beyond recognition and checks on political power like the judiciary and the press brought under their control, political leaders were free to plunder public funds, encouraged, as we have explained, by leading western concession seekers. A pattern of reckless corruption thus quickly developed led by the rulers and their immediate supporters. Other subordinates, who came to feel that being honest left them hungrier and open to abuse, all joined in so that rabid corruption was everywhere evident and became virtually legitimized as no one was punished for it.

Consequence of Political and Economic Malaise

The consequences of the political and economic problems discussed above were dire. Political leaders set up one party states, outlawing the opposition. Arguably, a one party government can be a vehicle for unity in extremely fractious multi-ethnic societies. Arguments like this were put forward by political leaders like Julius Nyerere of Tanzania and Nkrumah of Ghana to justify some of the earliest one party states established in the 1960s. Some of the political leaders setting up these one party states were genuinely interested in using them for such expressed purposes. Others only wanted this as a means of destroying the opposition.

In the face of these developments, political instability began to manifest itself in various states on the African continent. One aspect of this instability was seen in military coup d'états, where the military, whose leaders had usually been appointed by the head of state, used its muscle to get rid of the President and his government and establish itself as the new rulers. Military coups erupted as early as 1962 in Togo and the President Sylvanus Olympio was assassinated in the process. In 1965, President Yameogo of Upper Volta (Burkina Faso) was replaced by the military. There were military coups in Nigeria and Ghana in 1966 followed by a protracted civil war in Nigeria. Coups occurred in several countries and repeatedly in countries like Nigeria and Ghana and Sierra Leone. Such take over of governments can be counted in various parts of the continent including Sudan, Ethiopia, the Congo and Uganda.

Military coups were sometimes initially welcome by the population which regarded them as quick remedies to remove what had often become unpopular governments that seemed impossible to get rid of. The expectation was that soldiers would use their military might to enforce free and fair elections and then return to their barracks. Things never quite worked out that way. It was very tempting for the military to use its guns to hold on to power and use obvious force to keep every one in tow. Thus military leaders began to convert their military positions into political ones, some also establishing one party states in the process. This happened in cases like those of Mobutu Sese Seko of Zaire (now Democratic Republic of the Congo), with Flight-lieutenant Jerry Rawlings of Ghana, Lansana Conte of Guinea and Samuel K. Doe of Liberia. The records of military leaders turned Presidents were similar to their civilian counterparts. They invariably turned rich and corrupt and persecuted any opposition that appeared in their countries.

Alternative Political Philosophies—African Socialism

Some of the African heads of states attempted to develop patterns of government based on what they believed were visions different from the colonial heritage and more adaptable to the African condition. In this regard, various expressions and interpretations of 'African socialism' seemed attractive to African leaders.

The idea of African socialism was attractive because of its association with the Marxist-Leninist socialism practiced by the Soviet Union and its eastern European allies. The idea of rejecting class domination in society, which was seen as a cornerstone of the colonialist, capitalist economies that had exploited Africa, appeared the best thing. Besides, it was believed that this prevention of control by a rich capitalist class was similar to traditional African values. While some African rulers merely used this as rhetoric, others believed they could combine this Marxist and African socialist values into a workable system that would redeem African countries.

The outcomes were less hopeful than any of these rulers would have imagined. Kenya tried a version of African socialism that was not clearly articulated. Within a few years the President Jomo Kenyatta and his finance minister, Tom Mboya, were admitting that this classless society was not working.

President Sekou Touré of Guinea developed his own brand of African socialism. His radical break with France had left the latter hostile to Guinea and Sekou Touré spent far more of his concern on internal security than on developing an economy based on socialist principles. He however nationalized banks, insurance companies and manufacturing to prevent dominance by a few rich private interests. But farmers were not happy with state dominance of agriculture in collectivized farms and their lack of support affected Touré's economic policies. Touré also worked closely with the Soviet Union and China, both of which helped with mining bauxite and new techniques for growing rice respectively. Before Sekou Tourê died in 1984 however, he had begun to court western investment that had been markedly absent from Guinea.

In Ghana, President Kwame Nkrumah's brand of African socialism did not admit of any classless society in traditional Africa. Nkrumah based his African socialism on Marxist-Leninist principles. Though he did not nationalize key industries, he created 'parastatals,' part government controlled organizations for running major sectors of the economy. With an economy dependent primarily on the export of cocoa, Nkrumah retained the colonial system of a state controlled marketing system that paid the farmers a lower price for their cocoa, the state retaining the difference. By the time Nkrumah was overthrown in 1966, the price of cocoa had fallen drastically on the world market, adversely affecting Ghana's economy.

Variants of African socialism were tried in other African countries like Senegal and Zambia but the most articulated and talked about was that of Julius Nyerere of Tanzania. Nyerere's version of African socialism was embodied in his policy of *ujaama*, the Kiswahili word for family. Unlike Nkrumah, Nyerere believed that indigenous African societies were classless, where no one exploited the other. The largely rural nature of Tanzanian society made Nyerere believe he could build a new brand of classless society in Tanzania.

Nyerere's principles of African socialism were set forth in a document called the Arusha Declaration, named after the town where the momentous meeting was held outlining the policies. Major industries were nationalized and rules were set to ensure that top party people like ministers and bureaucrats did not use their positions to enrich themselves. They could not own shares in industry nor more than one home. In order to develop the rural economy and infrastructure, Nyerere attempted to bring together many small rural settlements into larger, more viable *ujaama* settlements so that elements like schools and water supply could be more meaningfully brought to these larger units. These *ujaama* settlements would then become major units, making economic and political changes to affect their own destinies.

Nyerere's plans however fell on rocky ground. Local people, tied to their ancestral lands, resented the idea of being ordered to move to 'new' areas. A border war with Uganda took a heavy economic toll while the oil price hikes of the 1970s and successive droughts hit Tanzania particularly hard. In 1973 alone, for example, Tanzania had a combination of bad harvests, marked increases in world prices for grain, oil, fertilizers and manufactured goods, while there was at the same time a sharp decline in the world prices of commodities that Tanzania exported. For a long time Nyerere refused to succumb to the demands of structural adjustment policies provided by the World Bank with all its 'conditionalities' we will discuss subsequently. This meant that little or no foreign monies were coming into Tanzania, and Nyerere was accused of failed policies adopted against western warnings. Nyerere resigned in 1985 but is well remembered for genuine efforts to lift his people out of economic backwardness.

All of these policies of African socialism failed. But all of the leaders discussed above were Presidents genuinely concerned with finding a viable system of government adaptable to the African indigenous condition and the need for development. They were opposed to corruption and none of them enriched himself or died wealthy. However, in order to control potentially destructive ethnicity and provide a political system stable enough to pursue policies based on their perceptions of meaningful change, these leaders had believed that a more autocratic system of government was necessary. But while they created mass parties, the combination of one party governments and autocratic rule did not lend itself to the kind of progress they wanted. Thus the leadership of mass parties gradually lost touch with the people and the policies failed.

Various brands of governments, basically capitalist and following the western economic system, were more prevalent in other African countries.

The most important distinction is that many of them became one party governments where this system was basically used to keep the leaders in office and use state resources to enrich them and their immediate followers.

Declining Economies and External Assistance

As the political systems of African countries weakened, their economies were simultaneously deteriorating. The inability of a corrupt government to impose its will on its immediate followers engaging in similar practices simply made this corruption the order of the day. This filtered into every area of the bureaucracy and politics. It simply provided the best avenues for foreign interests to siphon off the wealth of the countries either in mineral or other resources as corrupt officials virtually gave away these concessions. The interests of the great majority of the population were therefore neglected so that poverty, hunger and desperation became more rampant, a very good prescription for rebellions and civil wars.

To stave off these disasters, African countries began to depend increasingly on foreign assistance from the developed world in the form of loans, grants and aid, much of which was provided through or with the cooperation of the International Monetary Fund (IMF) and the World Bank, institutions of the United Nations dominated by the powerful western countries.

The IMF and the World Bank

These two institutions, set up through the United Nations as a way of assisting member countries in difficult times, have had a tremendous influence on the economies of poor African countries. It is clear to some Africans that these are instruments of the western countries, used to tie African countries more securely to the global economic system as powerless appendages that could be more readily exploited.

These institutions had already been 'snooping' in African countries under colonial rule, contrary to the popular belief that the IMF and World Bank only started providing 'assistance' to African countries in their post-independence economic downturn. A World Bank mission was invited to Nigeria in 1953 by the British colonial government, to advise on the Nigerian economy. It is clear that Nigeria's first Development Plan for 1962–68 was based on the report of the World Bank mission and it was drafted by two Americans. In this and other ways, the IMF and World Bank helped establish the colonial economic design of keeping African countries as primary producers of raw materials, their argument being that Africans had a comparative advantage producing and selling these primary products. The groundwork for misguiding the African economies by these western controlled institutions in the post-colonial era had in fact been laid when these African states were still colonies.

Export of these primary products by African countries has been declining as mentioned earlier, due to a combination of factors. These include the low and continuously falling prices imposed by the developed world for these products. There were also other trade practices of the developed world that were unfavorable to African countries like tariff barriers on the exports from developing countries. By the end of the twentieth century, for example, extremely high tariff was imposed on manufactured products from developing countries including African states entering the markets of industrialized countries. Such tariff was on average four times higher than those imposed on similar goods from other industrialized countries. On the other hand, developed countries subsidize the export of surplus food products of their own farmers, thus helping these farmers to dump cheap food in poor countries. This of course threatens the livelihood of poor developing country farmers who could not compete to sell their products in their own countries. Industrialized countries also use synthetics as substitutes for some of the products of African countries, reducing the need and so the demand and price of these primary products. These and other factors combined meant that African earnings from selling their primary goods declined sharply. For example, African countries are estimated to have lost a total of US $19 billion in export earnings between 1985 and 1986 alone as a result.

As the African economies suffered, they increasingly began to turn to the IMF and World Bank for financial support by the late 1970s. It was about this time, when European nations were now borrowing very little, that the Structural Adjustment Programs (SAP), the harsh pre-conditions for lending by the IMF, began to be enforced by this institution. These pre-conditions, referred to as 'conditionalities,' usually included insistence on devaluation of the currency, large scale retrenchment of workers, removal of restriction on trade and the lowering of tariffs which would benefit foreign capital interests, privatization of public enterprises thus removing any state controls, free entry of MNCs, lifting of price, wage and exchange controls, budget cuts, sometimes even reduction of the size of the government. After 1990, insistence on liberal democratic reform was added, as if this were a panacea of all political ills.

These conditionalities were never in the interest of the African countries which had been pushed by dire economic circumstances to seek IMF and World Bank loans. In most African countries, for example, the government is the largest employer. Essential goods like gasoline, consumer goods, often even staple diet like rice or maize meal, are often heavily subsidized by government. If wages are frozen and subsidies on essential goods removed, the price of such goods would skyrocket beyond the means of the average wage earner whose wage was already low. In fact a good number of these wage earners would have lost their jobs through retrenchment, considerably worsening their purchasing power in a situation where there were no welfare benefits. Trade liberalization and tariff restructuring were generally geared towards the influx into these African countries of manufactured goods from the western countries which particularly the western oriented African urban middle class believed were necessary. This of course would stifle any industrialization efforts of these African countries.

The IMF applied these conditionalities to all African countries, irrespective of the individual nature of their economies. African countries had to accept these pre-conditions otherwise the IMF or any other foreign country or institution from the western would not lend any money to that African country. For western economic interests and governments increasingly tied their financial aid to African countries to compliance with IMF prescriptions.

Monitoring the imposition of these conditionalities meant literally taking over the economies of these poor countries. Officials in Zaire complained that their finance ministry and central bank had been taken over by the IMF, while late President Nyerere accused these institutions of attempting an economic re-colonization of Africa. These conditionalities of the SAPs only grew stiffer as African countries inevitably became more deeply indebted and needed more assistance from the same sources. 35 sub-Saharan countries adopted 162 World Bank/IMF adjustment programs since 1981, compared to only 126 SAPs in the rest of the world. Of course the mass of the population reacted to the implementation of these conditionalities with rebellion. Rice riots occurred in Zambia and Liberia, for example. There were demonstrations and national debates as in Nigeria over the validity of the roles of the IMF and World Bank in Africa. Some countries tried to abandon SAPs because of the serious social strife they generated. Senegal attempted this in 1984, Mali in 1986 and 1987. This abandonment of SAPs resulted in an immediate stoppage of all international financial assistance to these countries. They were thus forced to quickly restore the SAPs.

The World Bank, which was more concerned with rural development, seemed more interested in boosting agricultural development, largely to increase production for export. Huge loans were given to African countries to boost agriculture and promote development including marketing strategies, farm-to-market roads, rural water supply and other areas. These loans were largely controlled by companies selected by the funding agency. The purchase of machinery and contracts to build pre-fabricated infrastructure to support the project were issues decided by the World Bank agents. Integrated Agricultural Development Projects (IADPs as they were called), funded by the World Bank, lasted five to ten years and provided largely demonstration effect. Their sustainability in terms of maintaining the structures and providing the chemical fertilizers, improved roads on a continuing basis were never a major concern. At the end of these projects, the African countries fell more into debt with little to show for it. When all of these failed, the African countries were always the only ones responsible, always to blame for advice and strategies planted on them by the same western controlled agencies which gave them the loans.

And yet African countries kept taking these loans, even soliciting them as quickly as the agencies were willing to give them. The dominant thinking frame of the African political leaders and administrators who gladly accepted these projects also included the mistaken idea touted by the lending agencies, that these projects were good for the African countries. Any reflexive administrator or Minister who deigned to object to these projects was sidetracked by the lending agencies and their African supporters, who often then conspired to get such recalcitrants removed from office. The focus on SAPs also meant a lack of attention to social functions like healthcare and education which consequently suffered.

The Foreign Debt

In ways such as these, but also including corruption disproportionate to the small African economies, African countries fell into massive foreign debt. The debt burden was multiplied by increasingly unfavorable interest rates, particularly in the 1980s. Servicing this debt became a major part of the economies of these African countries. This only served to increase the strangle hold of the western capitalist countries over these African countries through the IMF and World Bank

The debt grew so large that it was estimated by the year 2000 that every person in these indebted African countries owes an average of $573 to their western creditors. Between 1980 and 1986, external debt of countries in Africa south of the Sahara rose from US $55.7 to US $102 billion. By the year 2000, some forty percent of African government revenues were directed towards servicing a total debt of $350 billion. Many African countries were now spending a good chunk of their meager resources servicing debt, often merely paying the interest on this debt to the neglect of social services like education and health. It is estimated that by 1989, debt servicing by sub Saharan African countries had risen to a combined figure of US $17.8 billion. There were as many as 32 re-scheduling of debt repayments before the mid 1980s as African countries could not meet existing schedules. Many new loans began to go right back to debt servicing rather than to benefit the economies of the recipient countries. African countries were thus caught in a bind from which they could not extricate themselves. With paltry resources and debt servicing, most African countries have become economically and politically worse off after all of the IMF 'assistance.'

By the year 2000, there have been debt relief initiatives by the developed countries for the heavily indebted poor countries (HIPCs) most of which are African. Much of the proposals on paper significantly reduce the debt for many countries. When related to what these countries would have left to spend on education and health services, the proposals are very meager. In addition, these proposals are hemmed in with IMF conditionalities, making it difficult for many countries to accept even this limited initiative.

Recent IMF and World Bank Initiatives—Poverty Reduction Strategies

By the year 2000, a new strategy adopted by the IMF and World Bank was to require each low income borrowing government to work with its citizens, but also with donors and creditors to develop a Poverty Reduction Strategy Paper (PRSP). This is supposed to be a three-year national development strategy with an emphasis on the participation and interest of borrowing countries. The PRSP had to be endorsed by the IMF and World Bank and this would qualify the government to receive loans, grants and debt relief.

The PRSP virtually replaced development plans of these governments, programs developed by a government and its citizens and approved by its parliament. And yet the IMF and World Bank made disbursement of loans and debt relief contingent upon their approval of such a plan involving all government programs. This gave these institutions virtual control of the design of all government plans.

In the case of Ghana, an interim PRSP had to be first prepared for approval by the IMF and World Bank This interim document contained a 'policy matrix,' a list of policy conditions that the country had to accept. These were prepared by the IMF and World Bank and inserted into the interim PRSP without the parliament of Ghana or the government having considered them.

The prescriptions of the interim PRSP reversed commitments the Ghana government had made to its people a few months before its last presidential elections. These commitments included export subsidies on cocoa, Ghana's chief export, and tariff measures to provide temporary protection for Ghana produced textiles, processed agricultural goods and a few other staples like toothpaste and soap. These commitments had been made against a background of stiff competition the Ghana producers faced from similar imported goods from the developed world entering Ghana at low tariffs, and these low tariff measures were adopted on IMF strictures. Forcing needy governments to abandon these commitments to their populace therefore amounts to encouraging autocratic attitudes by helpless governments against their peoples, while the IMF had often talked about encouraging democracy in these countries.

In some countries like Tanzania, the IMF had already approved the country's programs of spending before the PRSP was to come into effect, so that the PRSP would have little effect. These lending agencies have in effect only been dressing their old tactics in new clothing, continuing to strangle the development of these poor countries, yet mounting a media campaign to present countries complying with its impositions as progressive.

Questions

1. What motivated some African leaders to seek different political strategies to govern the newly independent African states?
2. Evaluate the role of international financial assistance in the political economy of African countries.

Chapter XIII
೫೦෬

Inter- and Intra-State Politics in Africa in the late Twentieth Century

There have been, in the post-colonial era, attempts by African countries to resolve thorny internal affairs and also issues resulting from contact between neighboring states by meetings and consultations between African states. Much of this cooperation moved towards the formation of an Organization for African Unity (OAU) in 1963 which provided the framework for cooperation between African states. Limited in scope, the OAU provided unity and support for the anti-colonial struggle in the remaining colonies in Africa. It was far more difficult for the OAU to intervene in internal struggles or in fractious neighborly relations between African states. In the area of economic cooperation, limited resources and jealous interests balked efforts at closer cooperation.

As the political situation deteriorated in certain countries and regions of Africa, smaller groups of countries and more regional organizations became more forceful in attempting to resolve conflicts. These conflicts, more intense in some areas than other, spawned excessive violence and genocide, aggravated famine and dispersed refugees widely across the continent. Hostilities continue to destabilize certain states and regions at the close of the twentieth century. We will look at these developments in turn.

Emergence of the Organization
for African Unity (OAU)

One of the primary figures in the quest for a united African government
was Kwame Nkrumah of Ghana. We have, in chapter nine, indicated his
background, including active participation in the Manchester Conference
of 1945. On the eve of Ghana's independence, Nkrumah declared that the
independence of Ghana would be meaningless without the independence of
all of Africa. He announced his intention to call a meeting of all self-
governing states in Africa.

That meeting took place in Accra, the capital of Ghana in April 1958
and was attended by representatives from Egypt, Ethiopia, Liberia, Libya,
Morocco, Sudan, Tunisia and of course Ghana. Apartheid South Africa was
invited but declined to attend. Resolutions were passed on a wide range of
economic and social matters, with much discussion on the African
personality. There was however a marked emphasis on the issue of guarding
the sovereignty of each state while the convener, Nkrumah, was clearly
interested in political unity as the basis of Africa's advancement.

Nkrumah forged ahead with his determination by calling in December
of 1958 an All Africa People's Conference (AAPC) in Accra. Invited were
prominent representatives of African countries already independent as well
as those still under colonial rule. Noticeably absent was the RDA party of
the French colonies, obviously from fear of the French. Prominent figures
from the diaspora were represented and the African-American veteran,
W.E.B. Dubois, then ninety-one, sent a speech that was read at the conference.

The delegates agreed to set up a permanent organization that would,
among other things, 'develop feeling of one community to assist the
emergence of a United States of Africa.'

This 1958 meeting helped precipitate the independence of a number of
African colonies as their delegates returned, fired with enthusiasm and
determination to work towards self rule for their territories. Two weeks
before this AAPC meeting, Nkrumah and Sekou Toure of Guinea had formed
a Ghana-Guinea union as a nucleus of a united Africa. Nkrumah had come
to Guinea's rescue as the French pulled out from Guinea everything possible
to give Guinea independence after Guinea opposed de Gaulle's constitution
for the French Community. The fanfare of the announcement of this union
between Ghana and Guinea and Nkrumah's persistent harping on African
political unity began to disturb those African leaders not particularly
interested in political unity. One of these leaders, President Tubman of

Liberia, then called a meeting on his home turf with Nkrumah and Sekou Toure, a meeting attended by George Padmore, Nkrumah's advisor. The compromise conclusion from this meeting was for an 'Associated States of Africa.' The participants then proposed, along those lines, for another meeting of independent African states to be held in Ethiopia in 1960.

Before this proposed meeting, the AAPC held another conference in Tunis in January 1960. While Ghana's proposals for political union were rejected, the conference agreed for the setting up of common institutions for economic, trade union and other cultural cooperation between African states. The meeting of independent African states met as planned in Ethiopia in June 1960 and at this meeting it became clear that there was a division between African leaders into moderates opposed to political unity, and the united Africa enthusiasts. Nkrumah was attacked by a Nigerian delegate for planning to impose himself as ruler of all of Africa. The conference rather moved towards emphasizing the existing boundaries of African states.

In a speech to his parliament in Ghana after this meeting, Nkrumah denounced supporters of a loose economic cooperation that resulted from the Addis Ababa Congress. This only hardened the rift between the opposing groups. The upheaval following the independence of the Congo and the resultant cold war played out there made Nkrumah strengthen his cries for African unity to tackle such problems. After meetings in Brazzaville (Congo) and Casablanca (Morocco) in January 1961, the two factions came to be labeled the Brazzaville and the Casablanca groups. The Brazzaville group, opposed to closer unity, was predominantly Francophone but had excluded Togo, Guinea and Mali and the North African Francophone countries. The Casablanca group, which met later, also excluded some countries, notably those of the Brazzaville group. Those who attended the Casablanca meeting included King Hassan of Morocco, President Nasser of Egypt, Nkrumah from Ghana, Sekou Toure of Guinea and Modibo Keita of Mali. This latter had joined Ghana and Guinea in what became the short lived Mali Federation. The Brazzaville group also met again in Monrovia, Liberia in May 1961.

The next two years witnessed strenuous efforts to reconcile differences between the two groups by leaders from opposing camps like Senghor of Senegal and Sekou Touré of Guinea. In the end, each group overlooked differences and agreed to a meeting of heads of states in Addis Ababa on 22 May 1963, the foundation of the Organization of African Unity (OAU). Though Nkrumah still enthusiastically called for political unity at the conference, his petulant attitude had antagonized others and he lost out on this issue.

Apart from a common anti-colonial stance as already mentioned, the OAU has been plagued by disagreement on most disputes between African states obviously due to varied interests over such a large continent. Regional organizations appear to have scored better success in mediating disputes. This is more especially true of the Economic Community of West African States (ECOWAS). While ECOWAS has not brought the economic systems of West African states much closer together, it has considerably eliminated barriers to travel between West African states for example. ECOWAS has also intervened in two West African civil wars and inter-state relations between Sierra Leone and Liberia.

African State Conflicts

Conflicts within and between some African states have been prominent since the 1960s. In the past decade of the 1990s, such conflicts have flared into civil wars and genocide in countries such as Somalia, Ethiopia, Sudan, the Congo, Rwanda, Burundi, Liberia, Sierra Leone and Uganda. Some of these wars have a long history of deep- seated rifts between major segments of the population in each country. The civil wars in Angola and Mozambique, for example, are carry-overs from their late colonial past when these countries had to wage liberation wars against the Portuguese imperial ruler.

In Angola, the ruling Popular Movement for the Liberation of Angola (MPLA) had Marxist leanings and attracted Soviet and Cuban support at certain stages of the struggle. In the period of the cold war, this provided a convenient excuse for apartheid South Africa and the US to support dissident movements, one of which, the National Union for the Total Independence of Angola (UNITA) has remained as a military force fighting the MPLA government. UNITA leader, Jonas Savimbi, has reneged on any agreement that has been signed to end the war. Control of Angola's diamond mining has enabled Savimbi to continue the war after losing South African and US assistance at the end of the cold war.

Let us take a look at some of the major trouble areas.

The Great Lakes Crisis

Developments in the region around Lake Victoria/Nyanza involved political crises which came to engulf the surrounding nations of Rwanda, Burundi, Uganda and Democratic Republic of the Congo, formerly called Zaire. The developments involved primarily the peoples of Rwanda and Burundi, those described as Hutu and Tutsi. While these two came to be regarded as ethnic groups, they are historically the same people, sharing a single language called Kinyarwanda. Hutu and Tutsi are found in sizeable numbers in Uganda and Zaire where they largely arrived as refugees from Rwanda and Burundi.

The international community is familiar with these two groups through the media coverage of pogroms particularly in Rwanda in 1994 and similar destruction surrounding the ousting of President Mobutu Sese Seko of Zaire in 1996. This has been presented as ethnic conflict in Africa, implying two peoples fighting each other particularly because of ethnic hostility. As some observers have seen, this war was particularly a political struggle for power as happens in many other areas outside Africa. One analyst, Catherine Newbury, comments that rulers of states of this nature realize that

> Losing power entails heavy costs and therefore, to retain control, those in power often go to extreme lengths to undermine all opposition. One of the most common political tools at their disposal is to revive ethnic identities and try to set ethnically defined categories in opposition against each other.

Origins of the Crisis

The background to this crisis is traceable to colonial rule where Belgium inherited the tiny colonies of Rwanda and Burundi from Germany, after the latter lost the First World War. The Belgian colonial rulers promoted the cattle keeping Tutsi, a tiny minority, above the much larger Hutu farmers. This favor of the Tutsi was related to some mythical sense of superiority of the Tutsi created by early western scholars who saw in the Tutsi some western physical traits. The Tutsi were thus dominant throughout the colonial period but towards the end of colonial rule, particularly in Rwanda, the departing Belgians moved to surrender control to the majority Hutu. Consequent social tensions led to what came to be called a 'social revolution,' starting in 1959. This established Hutu supremacy and in the process, hundreds of Tutsi were massacred. Thousands of Tutsi then fled Rwanda to seek asylum in neighboring countries, especially in Uganda. Rwandan refugees in Uganda and Zaire were not only Tutsi. Land pressure in Rwanda meant that also Hutu had over the years migrated to these neighboring countries. By the 1980s, the number of Rwandan refugees in the neighboring countries was estimated at between 400,000 and 600,000.

In Rwanda, there were differences and alliances that separated the Hutu of the south from those of the north. The southern Hutu had retained political

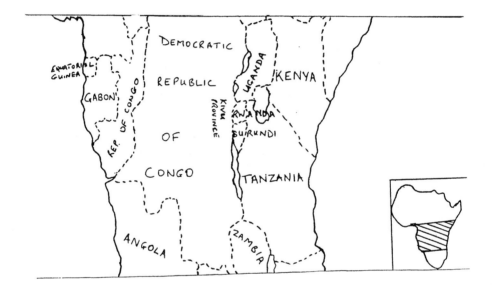

Democratic Republic of Congo and Great Lakes Region

control after independence in 1961 but a military coup d'etat of 1973 put the northern Hutu in power under a new leader, Habyarimana. The northern Hutu were determined to consolidate power as against those of the south who had hitherto dominated office. Hutu politicians mostly from the south and central who were in prison at the time were mysteriously slaughtered and Habyarimana's government was believed responsible. Other opponents of the government were equally eliminated. This was clearly not a Hutu/ Tutsi conflict.

The Habyarimana government had no intention of allowing the descendants of earlier Rwandan refugees living in Uganda or Zaire to return home. This may have been for political reasons or land inadequacy. These Rwandan refugees, particularly those in Uganda, suffered the disadvantage of being treated as refugees in Uganda as well as not being allowed to return to Rwanda which they considered home. In fact in 1982 the Ugandan government under President Obote expelled thousands of Rwandans from Uganda and many of these were kept in refugee camps in Rwanda for up to three years.

Some of the Rwandan refugees did well in Uganda and a number of them joined Yoweri Museveni's National Resistance Army (NRA) that eventually overthrew the second regime of President Obote in Uganda. This gave them some clout in Uganda, and this probably played into later developments in Rwanda. After the NRA removed Obote from office, Rwandans in Uganda, including those who had been part of the NRA, formed a Rwandan Patriotic Front (RPF) which launched an invasion of Rwanda in October 1990. President Mseveni of Uganda has been charged with fore knowledge of this plan in which many leading Rwandans of his NRA played a part.

The rebel RPF army quickly reached Kigali, the Rwandan capital, and Habyarimana's government was only saved by Belgian and French forces sent to Kigali ostensibly to protect foreigners. This foreign support strengthened the Habyarimana regime. Tutsi in Rwanda were killed in reprisals following the invasion as the rebels were mostly Tutsi. Fighting between the RPF and the government of Habyarimana continued intermittently until 1992.

In the midst of this fighting, Habyarimana was pressured into loosening up the political system in Rwanda to allow more political parties other than the ruling *Mouvement National pour la Révolution et le Développement* (MNRD). This development only strengthened hard liners in the MNRD who saw possible alliance between the RPF and some of the new opposition parties, particularly those that were ethnically mixed and included southern Hutu. These extremists saw this possible development as a threat to northern Hutu rule and felt assured in this fear when an agreement was reached in 1993 in Arusha to end the war and share power between the MNRD and the RPF in particular. As the Arusha negotiations continued and soon after the signing of the accord, mass killings occurred and evidence was available that these were either organized by or instigated by the Habyarimana regime in order to sustain Hutu-Tutsi antagonisms. The international community, particularly the Belgians and French present at the capital, and representatives of the United Nations, did nothing in the face of these persistent organized massacres even when the evidence pointed clearly to the MNRD regime. In fact France kept increasing its military assistance to the MNRD regime.

To aggravate the situation, in October 1993, President Ndadaye, the first Hutu president of neighboring Burundi, was assassinated in a coup d'etat by an army that was almost entirely Tutsi. The Tutsi had been hitherto dominant in Burundi and had mercilessly suppressed the Hutu until Ndadaye won elections early in 1993. His demise was interpreted by the Hutu hardliners in Rwanda as a signal to massacre the Tutsi and Hutu opponents of the MNRD. The wave of Hutu/Tutsi violence that erupted in Burundi following the assassination of Ndadaye sent some 200,000 Hutu as refugees into southern Rwanda. This was exactly the area where the MNRD government wanted allies to move against the southern Hutu opponents of the Habyarimana regime. These fleeing Hutu from Burundi were readily mobilized by the MNRD government into several militias to massacre Tutsi and southern Hutu.

The signal for the massacres came with the shooting down of Habyarimana's plane in April 1994. While those responsible for this are unknown, the fingers point clearly to the hardliners in the MNRD who wanted to eliminate Habyarimana because he had signed the Arusha Accord and allowed multi party democracy. They could also easily blame this event on opponents of the MNRD who they now moved to eliminate en masse.

The killings in Kigali began soon after the plane crash. It is estimated that somewhere close to one million Rwandans, both Tutsi and Hutu, died in these macabre killings by the MNRD and their hired militia. The international community stood idly by with Belgium and France who were heavily represented at the Rwandan capital appearing not to understand what was going on. United Nations troops which had reached Kigali in November 1993 to help carry out the Arusha Accord claimed they had neither the resources nor the mandate to intervene.

Repercussions in the Congo

Since the early colonial period, many Hutu and Tutsi had been brought to work on European plantations in the eastern Congo, particularly its Kivu province that bordered Rwanda and Burundi. By the post-colonial era, these Hutu and Tutsi considered themselves Congolese. The Rwandan revolution of 1959-66 had brought in many new Tutsi and Hutu refugees to Kivu. Similar migrations from Burundi to the Congo had occurred particularly in 1972 after a failed Hutu uprising and a savage exaction of vengeance by an all Tutsi army in Burundi. These newer Hutu and Tutsi refugees in Kivu had entrenched themselves, buying land which was increasingly becoming a scarce resource.

As Hutu and Tutsi became prosperous in the Congo, they came to be increasingly considered as foreigners by the indigenous Congolese (or Zairois as they were regarded at the time). Up to the 1980s, a law in Zaire had recognized Hutu and Tutsi in the Kivu Province and elsewhere in Zaire as citizens of that country. But a new law of 1981 literally stripped them of this citizenship. This decision began to bring Hutu and Tutsi in Zaire closer together for a common cause. They were however separated again after the genocide in Rwanda in 1994 and the resultant flight of over one million Hutu from Rwanda into the Kivu and surrounding provinces in the Congo. Hutu and Tutsi labels became important again in Zaire and the Rwandan genocide began to find a new ground in Hutu and Tutsi reprisals on each other in the Kivu area. Major massacres of Tutsi by Hutu militia occurred in north and south Kivu, with the full backing of the local authorities in Kivu.

The Rwandan government was drawn into this situation in Zaire and in October 1996, units of the Rwandan Patriotic Front army which had been integrated into the Rwandan government following the Arusha Accord launched attacks on refugee camps in Zaire where such camps bordered Rwanda and Burundi. Thousands were killed, hundreds of thousands further displaced, while similar numbers returned to their homeland of origin in Rwanda and Burundi.

In the midst of this affray emerged Laurent Kabila in Kivu at the head of an Alliance of Democratic Forces for the Liberation of the Congo (ADFL). A coalition of interests quickly developed. Kabila wanted to overthrow President Mobutu Sese Seko who had ruled Zaire for over twenty years, suppressing all opposition and propped up by US support due to US interest in the copper in Zaire. The Rwandan interests in Kivu were opposed to Mobutu for the growing move to render the Rwandans at Kivu as non-

Zairois. If they could get rid of Mobutu, they stood a good chance of keeping Kivu as a safe haven for Rwandans, a place that could become a launching pad against any unpopular Rwandan government.

While the ADFL/Rwandan insurgents moved towards Kinsasha, the Zaire capital and ousted Mobutu in 1997, other scores were being settled at the refugee camps in the Kivu area. Uganda was hunting elements of the Alliance of Democratic Forces (ADF) who were making hit-and-run attacks on Uganda from bases in north-eastern Congo (as Zaire now became after Kabila became ruler). The Burundi army was attacking the refugee camps in south Kivu from where dissidents had been launching attacks on Burundi. The Rwandan army was attacking the refugee camps in the area to get at Rwandan ex-military elements who were believed to be using these camps as bases for anti-Rwandan military activities. Waves of refugees were therefore sent back and forth between the Congo, Rwanda and Burundi, many returning to a homeland they rarely knew, many killed in the process. By the year 2000, the total number of refugees returning to Burundi, for example, was estimated at about 338,000.

The victorious Kabila in Kinsasha, the capital of the Democratic Republic of the Congo, the new name, proceeded to take high handed measures to clamp down on the opposition which had been resisting Mobutu. Many were arrested and jailed as Kabila dodged international accountability that was interested in investigating the pogroms against thousands of refugees fleeing the eastern Congo. Kabila however made the mistake of supporting anti-Tutsi sentiment in the Congo and moving against Tutsi elements in his army and administration. This set him on a collision course against the combined forces of Uganda and Rwanda, on which he had depended. This newly combined interest now spurned a massive rebellion in the eastern Congo in 1998. Dissidents in the eastern Congo were readily mobilized and an invading army moved towards the capital. Kabila was saved by Angolan troops that entered the Congo and pushed back the rebels.

The situation remained a virtual stalemate into the twenty first century. President Kabila has only been able to retain control of the Kasai diamond mines with military help from Angola and Zimbabwe, for which he has made mining concessions to Zimbabwe. The cost of the war has adversely impacted the economy of Zimbabwe where only powerful individuals seem to have benefited from these mining concessions. Early in 2001, Laurent Kabila was assassinated in a palace coup and replaced by his son, Joseph who had been head of his army.

Ethiopia

A few years after the end of the Second World War, Ethiopia was freed of British military occupation and was given control of Eritrea and other Ethiopian territory hitherto under British control. Problems however remained over Ethiopia's ability to centrally control all of these fragments of territory. By 1962, Ethiopia had used strong arm methods to dominate Eritrea which had remained an Italian, then British colony up to the 1950s and had thus developed a separate identity. Eritreans therefore eventually overcame their rivalries and banded together in a resistance movement which gained control of most of Eritrea by 1977.

The Eritrean rebellion also engulfed the Ethiopian province of Tigray where secessionist tendencies were also evident. In the Ogaden, another Ethiopian province dominated by people of Somali nationality, a Western Somali Liberation Front (WSLF) was raking up hostility over Ethiopia's control of the Ogaden and in this the WSLF was supported by the neighboring Somali government. This WSLF was also making large advances on Ethiopian territory; combined with the Eritrean and Tigray movements these spelled trouble for the Ethiopian government of Mengistu Haile Mariam in 1977. The Ethiopian government was only saved by the support of Soviet and Cuban troops who drove off the attackers, and with their support Ethiopia gained control of much of Eritrea again.

The Eritrea and Ogaden crises left their mark in a bitter power struggle at the Ethiopian capital in 1977–78 when Mengistu's forces launched a reign of terror in which thousands of Ethiopians lost their lives. This however did not save Mengistu. The Eritrean forces again overcame their differences and launched a major offensive against Ethiopia called Operation Red Star in 1982 in which the Ethiopian army lost thousands of its soldiers. Mengistu's policies, like the re-settlement in the south-west of 1.5 million peasants from the north, only deepened his woes. The army was unable to bring the Eritreans under control and lost heavily in men, arms and ammunition in a major offensive it launched against Eritrea in 1988.

Ethiopian opposition elements within the country including those from Tigray, now got together in a movement called the Ethiopian Peoples Revolutionary Democratic Front (EPRDF) which launched an assault on Mengistu's government. This, plus the Eritrean problem, led Mengistu to flee the country in 1991, leaving the EPRDF in control. This provisional EPRDF government had no choice but to concede to Eritrean demands for a referendum on independence. The results were overwhelmingly in favor of independence which came to Eritrea in May 1993.

Ethiopia never completely reconciled to the loss of Eritrea. Every reason was found to develop a dispute which led to the reopening of war between Ethiopia and Eritrea again in 1998. Thousands of Eritreans who were either born in or had lived in Ethiopia all their lives were 'expelled' from Ethiopia, to a homeland in Eritrea they knew little or nothing about. By the year 2000, Ethiopia had claimed victory when the fighting intensified and Ethiopian forces overran many towns in Eritrea.

Somalia

Conflict in Somalia derived from opposition to the Somali government by dissidents from the north of the country that had been British controlled. There was also the problem of the Ogaden which Somalia felt was hers since it was inhabited by mostly Somali nationals. But Britain gave control of the Ogaden to Ethiopia and this stirred up Somali hostility. In 1977, the Somali President, Siad Barre, sent forces to support the Somali rebels in the Ogaden against the Ethiopian government. This move, roundly condemned by the OAU, was unsuccessful as the Ethiopian government got relief from Soviet/Cuban intervention. Sporadic cross border attacks continued between Ethiopia and Somalia throughout the 1980s

A rapprochement was reached between these two countries in 1988 about problems across their common borders. This made it virtually impossible for the mostly northern dominated Somali National Movement (SNM) to continue operating from its former bases in Ethiopia. This movement now mobilized its forces from within Somalia and intensified its military attacks on the Somali government. A major thrust in 1988 led to heavy Somali government reprisals in which over 5,000 Somalis lost their lives and hundreds of thousands fled as refugees into neighboring countries or into other parts of Somalia as displaced persons.

Somalia under Siad Barre lost international financial support amidst claims of human rights abuses as thousands lost their lives in repression by the Barre regime. In 1990, Siad's forces fired at spectators who dared to jeer at the president at a stadium. This fueled more armed resistance that became threatening enough so that Siad had to flee the capital in January 1991.

A loosely organized coalition of the rebel groups calling itself the United Somali Congress (USC) took control of the capital but this soon split into two opposing factions. One of these factions, the northern-based SNM refused to recognize the government and declared the secession of the north.

The USC in Mogadishu, the capital, split along clan lines late in 1991 and the city became basically divided between the USC leader, Ali Mahdi and his former military commander, Mohammed Farrah Aideed. Factional fighting, supported by recurrent droughts plagued Mogadishu and the rest of Somalia as it became extremely difficult for international relief agencies to deliver supplies to starving Somalis.

Using United Nations agreement as a basis, US forces, joined by a few from other European nations moved into Mogadishu in 1992 in a bid to restore order. Calm came temporarily to Somalia until the UN force tangled with Aideed who felt they were entering into negotiations that would end up marginalizing him. The ensuing conflict led to an attempt to arrest Aideed and the pursuit left eighteen US soldiers dead and dragged through the streets of Mogadishu in October 1993 as US audiences watched from their TV sets at home. This prompted a withdrawal of the American forces in March 1994. Factional fighting and a lack of a central government in Mogadishu has remained the plague of Somalia.

The Sudan

As mentioned in chapter ten, British colonial policy had helped broaden the divide between the Islamic and Arab north in the Sudan and the non-Islamic, more traditional south that had been continuously moved in the direction of Christianity and western orientation. This rift had developed to such a degree that the south had rebelled against control by the north on the eve of independence in 1955, when it was clear that rulership of the Sudan would be in the hands of northern elements. A surrender of the rebelling southern soldiers had been arranged which simply emphasized the northern domination. Many southern Sudan leaders and peoples fled to neighboring countries and formed organizations for resistance. These were consolidated into the *Anya-Nya* movement that started armed resistance against the Sudan government in 1963.

In 1972, a compromise was worked out between President Nemeiri, who had assumed office as a military leader after a coup d'état in 1969, and the southern Sudan rebels. This agreement, hammered out in neighboring Addis Ababa, recognized the southern Sudan as an autonomous unit. It did not however address issues of different levels of development and the religious divide between the Islamic north and the southern Sudan. Succeeding events led the southern Sudan peoples to believe that President Nemeiri was abandoning the spirit of the Addis Ababa agreement and moving, like other presidents before him, to Arabise and exploit the southern Sudan. Tensions began mounting again and war was precipitated by Nemeiri's imposition of the *Sharia*, Islamic law, over the entire country. The leaders of the southern resistance again came together in the Southern People's Liberation Army (SPLA) and launched an offensive that soon took control of much of southern Sudan. Mounting opposition developed against Nemeiri's government as he appeared to be losing the war, and this at a time of a rapidly deteriorating economic situation in the Sudan. Nemeiri was consequently overthrown in a military coup d'état in 1985.

Neither successive governments after Nemeiri nor international mediation could solve the seemingly intractable differences between the north and the south of Sudan, differences that were fuelling the Sudan civil war. Meanwhile, a cycle of persistent droughts in the 1980s simply aggravated the situation, leaving most of the population at risk as international relief efforts were thwarted because of the fighting. By 1991, international relief agencies were estimating that eight to eleven million people were at risk of starvation. It is still hard to tell how many hundreds of thousands of Sudanese perished under the combined assault of war and drought. The refugee situation was aggravated in 1991 when victorious rebel forces in neighboring Ethiopia, grateful for the Sudan government's assistance, proceeded to drive out southern Sudanese soldiers and refugees from Ethiopia.

The government in the Sudan has lost much of its international support because of its hard line position. But the rebel opposition has not remained united enough to prosecute the war successfully. At the close of the century, the SPLA remained in control of much of the southern Sudan and the war, which continues to devastate the economy of the Sudan and prevent relief efforts for famine victims, continues.

Liberia and Sierra Leone

Civil war in Liberia spread into and engulfed neighboring Sierra Leone throughout the 1990s. It all started in Liberia with a successful military coup d'état which represented a reaction by the indigenous Liberians against over a century of domination by the Americo-Liberian settlers and their allies. But the leader of the coup-turned-president, Samuel Doe, became an authoritarian and corrupt leader and quickly lost what popularity he had at the start. A rebellion against him by Americo-Liberian elements, the main faction being led by Charles Taylor, gained momentum by the late 1880s and succeeded in ousting and killing Doe.

The Liberian civil war dragged on throughout the 1990s as no efforts at mediation worked. The Economic community of West African States (ECOWAS) put together a West African monitoring force (ECOMOG) following a ceasefire agreement and this force ended up trying to enforce the peace by fighting against the leading rebel leader, Charles Taylor. The ECOMOG force was using neighboring Sierra Leone as a launching pad for bombardment of Liberia and this angered Charles Taylor who promised to bring civil war to Sierra Leone.

Charles Taylor then secured the assistance of Burkina Faso, his ally, to sponsor a group of Sierra Leone dissidents and opponents of the Sierra Leone government and a rebel force emerged calling itself the Revolutionary United Front (RUF). First reports of armed clashes with the Sierra Leone government forces occurred in March 1991 across the common border between Sierra Leone and Liberia. By 1992, the RUF rebels had made significant advances into Sierra Leone and this spurned a military overthrow of the Sierra Leone government of President Joseph Saidu Momoh. The new military government set up failed to successfully prosecute the war and it is believed that the military coup that brought them to office had been arranged in collaboration with the RUF rebels.

Under pressure from international sources and local interest groups, the military government conducted elections in Sierra Leone in 1996 and handed over office to a newly elected government led by President Tejan Kabba. The new president apparently distrusted the army and, following IMF prescriptions, proceeded to reduce much of the privileges of the army. There was a resultant army revolt which ousted Kabba from office and the military invited the RUF rebels into a joint government of Sierra Leone. This lasted for eight months following which the ECOWAS forces of the ECOMOG came to President Kabba's rescue and drove out the military/ RUF junta from Freetown, the capital. While this reinstated President Kabba, it drove the rest of the army and the RUF into the interior to renew the civil war. The RUF and military rebels actually fought their way into Freetown in January 1999, baffling the ECOMOG forces who were now Kabba's only source of military support. Thousands of people lost their lives and property as the RUF rebels destroyed a good part of Freetown before they retreated from it under reinforced ECOMOG attacks.

More recently, the war has reached a stalemate after the RUF leader, Foday Sankoh, virtually reneged on a peace treaty that had been worked in Lome, capital of Togo in 1999. Sankoh was arrested and detained but the RUF has held ground against UN peacekeeping forces that appear uncertain whether to observe or enforce peace in Sierra Leone. Meanwhile the RUF remains in control of the diamond rich district of Kono in Sierra Leone and their mining activities provide resources for President Charles Taylor of Liberia, from which he keeps the RUF well armed.

Conclusion

This adumbration of trouble spots in Africa in the late twentieth century should not leave one to assume that there is civil war all over Africa. While economic problems are compounded by natural disasters like drought, in some areas where the political situation has resulted in civil war the problems have seemed intractable. There are however some other countries in Africa, grappling with economic difficulties and working out possible ways of addressing the political complex.

Questions

1. Why was an Organization of African Unity, not a united African government, a more practical arrangement soon after independence in Africa?
2. To what degree was ethnicity a factor of conflict in post-colonial Africa?

Appendix

African States, Their Colonial Names and Rulers

Country[1]	Colonial Name	Colonial Ruler[2]	Year of Independence
Algeria	Algeria	France	1962
Angola	Angola	Portugal	1975
Benin	Dahomey	France	1960
Botswana	Bechuanaland	Britain	1966
Burkina Faso (Upper Volta)	Upper Volta	France	1960
Burundi	(part of) Rwanda-Urundi	Germany Belgium	1962
Cameroon	French Cameroon British Cameroon	Germany Britain, France	1960
Cape Verde	Cape Verde Is.	Portugal	1975
Central African Republic	Ubanghi-Chari	France	1960
Chad	Chad	France	1960
Comoros	Comoros	France	1975
Congo	Congo	France	1960
Democratic Rep. Of Congo (Zaire) (Congo Kinshasa)	Belgian Congo	Belgium	1960
Côte d'Ivoire	Côte d'Ivoire (IvoryCoast)	France	1960

Country[1]	Colonial Name	Colonial Ruler[2]	Year of Independence
Djibouti	French Somaliland (later Afars and Issas)	France	1977
Egypt	Egypt	Britain	1922
Equatorial Guinea	Fernando Po & Rio Muni	Portugal	1968
Ethiopia	Ethiopia	Italy (briefly, 1935–42)	1942
Gabon	Gabon	France	1965
The Gambia	Gambia	Britain	1965
Ghana	Gold Coast	Britain	1957
Guinea	French Guinea	France	1958
Guinea-Bissau	Portuguese Guinea	Portugal	1974
Kenya	Kenya	Britain	1963
Lesotho	Basutoland	Britain	1966
Liberia		American Colonization Society	1847
Libya	Cyrenaica, Tripolitania Fezzan	Italy	1951
Madagascar	Madagascar	France	1960
Malawi	Nyasaland	Britain	1964
Mali	French Sudan	France	1960
Mauritania	Mauritania	France	1960
Morocco	Morocco	France	1956
Mozambique	Mozambique	Portugal	1975
Namibia	South West Africa	Germany South Africa	1990
Niger	Niger	France	1960

Country[1]	Colonial Name	Colonial Ruler[2]	Year of Independence
Nigeria	Nigeria	Britain	1960
Réunion	Réunion	France	
Rwanda	(part of) Rwanda-Urundi	Germany Belgium	1962
Sao Tome & Principe	Sao Tome & Principe	Portugal	1975
Senegal	Senegal	France	1960
Seychelles	Seychelles Is.	France	1976
Sierra Leone	Sierra Leone	Britain	1961
Somali Democratic Republic	Italian Somaliland British Somaliland	Italy, Britain	1960
SouthAfrica	Union of South Africa	Netherlands Britain	1910
Sudan	Anglo-Egyptian Sudan	Britain, Egypt	1956
Swaziland	Swaziland	Britain	1968
Tanzania	Tanganyika, Zanzibar	Britain	1961, 1963
Togo	Togoland	Germany French, English	1960
Tunisia	Tunisia	France	1956
Uganda	Uganda	Britain	1962
Western Sahara	Spanish Sahara Rio de Oro	Spain	(In dispute)
Zambia	Northern Rhodesia	Britain	1964
Zimbabwe	Southern Rhodesia	Britain	1980

[1]Some countries changed names more than once since independence. The current name is given first, then the former post-colonial name in parenthesis.
[2]Some colonies had more than one colonial ruler at different times. The first name given under 'colonial ruler' usually represents the original colonizer.

Select Bibliography

There are a large number of works on African Studies presenting differing perspectives on the colonial and post-colonial History of Africa. This introductory work will not attempt to address most of them. The intention in this bibliography is to provide a start for the reader, so that mostly general and regional histories are addressed.

Ajayi, J.F.A and M. Crowder *History of West Africa volume 2*. London and New York, Longman 1974

Amin, Samir, *Neo-Colonialism in West Africa*. (English trans.) Harmondsworth, 1973

Asante, S.K.B. *Regionalism and Africa's Development: Expectations, Reality and Challenges*. New York, St. Martins Press, 1997

Assensoh, J.B. *African Political Leadership: Jomo Kenyatta, Kwame Nkrumah and Julius K. Nyerere*. Florida, Krieger, 1998

Austen, Ralph, *African Economic History: Internal Development and External Dependency*. Westport, Heinemann, 1987

Bassey, Magnus. *Western Education and Political Domination in Africa*. New York, Bergin and Garvey, 1999

Birmingham, D. *The Decolonization of Africa* Athens, Ohio University Press, 1995

Boahen, A. A. (ed), *Africa Under Colonial Domination 1880-1935*. UNESCO General History of Africa volume VII. Berkeley, University of California Press 1985

Boahen, A.A. with J. Ajayi and M. Tidy, *Topics in West African History*. Essex, Longman 1986

Copson, R. *Africa's Wars and Prospects for Peace*. Armonck, N.Y. M.E. Sharpe, 1994

Crowder, M. *West Africa Under Colonial Rule*. London, Hutchinson 1968

Crowder, M. and O. Ikime, (eds) *West African Chiefs: Their Changing Status under Colonial Rule and Independence*. N.Y., Africana 1970

Crowder, M (ed) *Cambridge History of Africa c.1940–c.1975*. volume 8, Cambridge University Press, 1984

Davidson, Basil *Modern Africa: A Social and Political History* (third edition). New York, Longman 1994

Ellis, Stephen, *Africa Now: People, Policies and Institutions*. Westport, Heinemann 1996

Esedebe, P. *Pan-Africanism: The Idea and Movement 1776–1963*. Washington D.C. Howard University Press, 1982

Falola, T. (ed). *Tradition and Change in Africa: The Essays of J.F. Ade Ajayi* Trenton, New Jersey, Africa World Press, 2000

Fanon, Frantz, *Black Skin, White Masks*. London, Paladin, 1970

Fanon, Frantz. *The Wretched of the Earth*. (trans. by C. Farrington) London, Penguin, 1983

Fashole-Luke, E., R. Gray, A. Hastings and G. Tasie,(eds) *Christianity in Independent Africa* London, Rex Collings, 1978

Harbeson, J.W and I. Kimambo (eds). *East African Expressions of Christianity*. Athens, Ohio University press, 1999

Hargreaves, J. D. *Decolonization in Africa*. London and New York, Longman, 1988

Hopkins, A.G. 1973, *An Economic History of West Africa*. London, Longman 1973

Isaacman, A. and Richard Roberts (eds). *Cotton, Colonialism and Society in Sub-Saharan Africa*. Portsmouth, Heinemann, 1995

Issawi, C. *An Economic History of the Middle East and North Africa*. London, Cambridge University Press, 1982

Kwabena-Nketia, E. *The Music of Africa*. London, Golancz, 1975

Mazrui, Ali A. (ed), *Africa Since 1935* UNESCO General History of Africa, Volume VIII.Berkeley, University of California Press, 1993

M'Bokolo, E. *La Continent Convoité: L'Afrique au Xxe Siècle*. Paris and Montreal, Editions Etudes Vivantes, Coll. Axes Sciences Humaines 1980

Mkandawire T. and Bourenane, N. *The State and Agriculture in Africa*. Dakar, CODESRIA, 1987

Nnoli, O. *Ethnic Conflict in Africa*. Dakar, CODESRIA, 1998

Ogot, B.A. and J.A. Kieran, *Zamani: A Survey of East African History*. Nairobi, East Africa Publishing House, 1968

Ogot, B.A. *Hadith V. Economic and Social History of East Africa*. Nairobi, East African Literature Bureau, 1975

Ogot, B.A., *History and Social change in East Africa*. Nairobi, EAPH, 1976

Oliver, R. and G.N. Sanderson (eds). *Cambridge History of Africa, Volume VI* Cambridge University Press, 1985

Omer-Cooper, J.D. *History of Southern Africa*. Westport, Heinemann, 1994

Onimode, Bade, *The IMF, The World Bank and the African Debt Volume I, the Economic Impact*. London and New Jersey, Zed Books, 1989

Onwumechili, Chuku, *African Democratization and Military Coups*. Portsmouth, Heinemann, 1998

Palmer, R. and N. Parsons, *Roots of Rural Poverty in Central and Southern Africa*. London, Heinemann, 1977

Patton, Adel, *Physicians, Colonial Racism and Diaspora in West Africa*. Gainesville, University of Florida Press, 1996

Ranger, T.O. and O. Vaughan (eds), *Legitimacy and the State in Twentieth Century Africa*. London, Macmillan 1993

Richards, Paul, *Indigenous Agricultural Revolution in West Africa*. London, Hutchinson, 1985

Roberts, A. (ed), *Cambridge History of Africa, Volume VII*. Cambridge University Press, 1986

Rodney,Walter, *How Europe Underdeveloped Africa*. Washington D.C., Howard University Press, 1974

Spear, Thomas, and I. Kimambo (eds). *East African Expressions of Christianity*. Athens, Ohio University Press, 1999

Suret-Canale, J. *Essays on African history: From the Slave Trade to Neo-Colonialism*. Trenton, New Jersey, Africa World Press, 1988

Wa Thiongo, Ngugi. *Decolonizing the Mind: The Politics of Language in African Literature*. Westport, Heinemann, 1986

Williams, Patrick & Laura Chrisman (eds), *Colonial discourse and Post-Colonial Theory*. Hertfordshire, Harvester Wheatsheaf, 1994

Woodward, P. and M. Forsyth. *Conflict and Peace in the Horn of Africa*. Aldershot, Dartmouth Publishing Company, 1994

Index